But God...

Dare to Dream Again

Mimi Lowe

xulon PRESS

But God...
Dare to Dream Again
by Mimi Lowe

Printed in the United States of America

ISBN 9781498423199

Scripture quotations taken from the New King James Version (NKJV). Copyright © 1979, 1980, 1982 by Thomas Nelson, Inc. Used by permission. All rights reserved.

Scripture quotations taken from the New International Version (NIV). Copyright © 1973, 1978, 1984, 2011 by Biblica, Inc.™. Used by permission. All rights reserved.

Book cover design was created by Andrew Skivington.

www.xulonpress.com

Do you want hope? Do you want to believe that God really exists and that He can make a difference in your life? Then...read this book! You will come away not saying, "God why did this happen to me?" but rejoicing that in spite of all that the enemy did to try to destroy you, there is a way to overcome through His power. Yes, bad things happened, "But God ..."

—Paul L. Cox, Aslan's Place, Apple Valley, California.

This book is the amazing story of a little Chinese girl from Canada who overcame, by the grace of God, deep loneliness, nagging depression, dissociative disorder, family hatred, and deep emotional pain to become a mighty woman of God. I could not put this book down! It is a must read for those who need to be reminded that God is sovereignly in control and that He has a plan and a purpose for our lives, no matter what we have gone through.

—Pastor Rob Gross, Mountain View
Community Church, Kaneohe, Hawaii

When I read the story of Mimi's life, I could not put the book down. I was stunned by the background she shared in her poignant story. To know Mimi—her kindness and humility, her power and intercession, her discernment and joy—is to see firsthand the mighty God she serves.

Her life reflects someone who has given her all to Jesus and walks in true victory and freedom. It is an honor to serve God alongside her.

—Pastor Linda Hoyt, Eleventh Hour Church,
Hackettstown, NJ

This is an amazing story of how the overwhelming love of God turned a broken life into one of power and victory. With transparent honesty, Mimi describes a lifetime of setbacks that left her emotionally handicapped. Through a series of supernatural events, including the personal appearance of Jesus in her bedroom, her life was transformed. This book will fill you with hope that there is nothing that can separate you from God's love and healing power.

—Grant Mullen, MD, author of *Emotionally Free*

Mimi Lowe has been a friend, counsellor, and fellow warrior since we met her at Catch the Fire Toronto (formerly TACF—Toronto Airport Christian Fellowship) in 1996. Mimi has a strong prophetic gifting and seer anointing, and she is sensitive and obedient to Holy Spirit's leading. She is a faithful woman of God exhibiting a hunger to dive deeper into the realms of the Spirit and possessing a strong passion to see captives set free. Mimi will seek the Lord for others and is relentless at pursuing freedom for others yet does not cross boundaries. The Lord has equipped her with some powerful tools for healing the broken hearted and bringing liberty to lost souls. We have always found Mimi to be a safe place to share our hearts. We have witnessed and received powerful impartations from her and have been blessed to find inner healing and deliverance through her ministry.

She walks in a realm of power and authority that is not easily matched, and her love for the Lord is evident!

In the pages that follow, you will find the expression of a true heart that is willing to be transparent and open so that you can see her walk into freedom and hopefully experience liberty for yourself. She has walked a difficult walk, coming from much trauma, rejection, pain, and often being misunderstood, but out of the fire has emerged one who is not easily shaken because she knows her Lord.

—Larry & Jacqueline Pearson, Founders,
Lion Sword Communications, Ontario, Canada

Beginning in the Chinese culture of the Canadian Northwest in the 1940s, this is a heart-wrenching story of a Chinese girl who encounters abandonment, physical abuse, and illness and with them all visions of evil spiritual beings. Only through the sustaining presence of God is she able to survive and overcome. Today, Mimi, a gifted seer, devoted mother and grandmother, a prayer minister and good friend testifies to the reality of a present, miracle-producing Jesus wherever she goes.

Encouraging and inspiring, *But God...* is a book that I found hard to put down.

—Pastor Patti Velotta

Senior Pastor of Calvary Way International Fellowship,

author of *Immanuel: A Practicum*, seminar speaker

and trainer of the Immanuel Approach

Mimi shares her life story—from emotional "rags," through a difficult journey, to "riches" in Christ Jesus. The Holy Spirit broke through Mimi's wounded-ness and slowly, tenderly revealed Himself to her. There are many unanswered "whys" in Mimi's story, and there are also many surprising explanations. This is a message for all who need hope and reassurance. What becomes obvious is that God worked mightily and uniquely in Mimi's life. The life she thought lacked worth has been transformed. The message of Mimi's life is that God IS alive and that His work is supernatural and real.

—Rev. Arthur Zeilstra,

Founder of Cornerstone Christian Counselling Centre,

Kitchener, Ontario, Canada

Much gratitude and acknowledgment to my family and friends who have prayed for me as I agonized over this book.

Many thanks to those who have given of their finances and their time toward this project.

A special "thank you" to John Sandford for allowing me to use examples of their teachings on inner healing.

Thank you, Dori Harrell of Breakout Editing, for sensitivity and expertise.

Most of all, thank You, Holy Spirit, for my liberty and freedom that enabled me to write His story.

FOREWORD

As Mimi's daughter, I started writing this foreword with the idea that my mom has changed into the person I know her as today. The truth is, I think she has always been brave, strong, and trusted God, but she just did not know it. Many times, she would throw up her hands in frustration and allow things to happen because she did not know what to do. Whenever I asked the "what if" questions, she always said things would work out. Much to her amazement, God was always there to take care of us and to ensure our well-being. When we moved, Mom left with nothing but her two children and a suitcase. She had no money and no furniture. Despite her own fears, and with many people saying she could not do it, she found a job, rented an apartment, and enrolled my sister and me into school, all by herself. There were dark days and difficult times when we did not have money for rent, food, or clothes. I did not know it then, but there were many times when she was confused, alone, and scared.

Looking back over our lives now, it is easy to see how God was guiding and protecting us. He sent special people into our lives to give us advice, like her coworker who told her about a better neighborhood in which to raise her children. My mom worked constantly as a waitress so she could manage to put me through private school and still make ends meet. Even though I was attending private school with girls whose parents were brain surgeons and executive vice presidents, I would brag about how my mom could carry six full plates all the way up her arm while waiting on tables.

I don't think Mom would be who she is today without having been through all her struggles. The major thing that really changed in my mom was her knowledge of God. She is able to impart that knowledge to other people because she knows what it is like to think you are all alone. Generally, my mom was quiet, yet my friends loved to come over and talk to her because she was the one who listened and understood. God has taught my mom how to use the wonderful gifts He has given her, and she is using these gifts to minister to others around the world.

I am so proud of you, Mom.

Valerie Lowe Skivington

Table of Contents

Introduction

*T*here have been many moments in my life where I believed God could not fix me.

The Chinese family and culture I was born into, the effects of war, extended periods of silence, demonic attacks, and severe illnesses shaped a person who could barely cope with the simplest functions of society.

My heart would cry, "God, can I be normal for just one day, just to know what it is like?" I thought that was too much to ask of God. I wanted to live a peaceful life without tormenting thoughts thundering in my mind. I wanted to make sound decisions. I wanted the simple ability to communicate with others and to function without overwhelming fear, anxiety, and emotional pain. I wanted to experience a life free of shame, guilt, and feelings of worthlessness, insecurity, hopelessness, and despair. I felt as if I did not have a sense of identity. I felt that what I was asking God, He could not provide. I believed that my mountains could not be moved.

I have since discovered that not only can God fulfill our dreams and enable us to live lives of joy and peace, but He also far exceeds our expectations. Looking back on my life, I can say, "Eye has not seen, nor ear heard, Nor have entered into the heart of man The things which God has prepared for those who love Him" (1 Cor. 2:9).

I'm sharing my story because I'm living proof that God pursues us in our pain and brokenness. God wants to remove anything that prevents us from knowing Him more intimately.

MY CURRENT LIFE

Since 2002 I have traveled to different parts of the United States and Canada, Singapore, England, Switzerland, Australia, and India. These opportunities were made available to me as I served as part of a prayer team associated with Aslan's Place, based in Hesperia, California. I interned with this ministry learning about spiritual discernment and generational deliverance—God delivering believers from the consequences of ancestral iniquities, based on this scripture, Exodus 34:7: "keeping mercy for thousands, forgiving iniquity and transgression and sin, by no means clearing the guilty, visiting the iniquity of the fathers upon the children and the children's children to the third and the fourth generation."

Aslan's Place ministry has been life changing for me as well as for many others around the world. In 2008 the doors opened for me to go to Switzerland to speak about spiritual discernment, generational deliverance, and prayer. However, this time I would be on my own, and public speaking is not my forte. I stayed with a pastor and his wife and three children for ten days. I had no other team member with me—only God. This would not have been possible for me to do even two years previously because overwhelming fear would have gripped and debilitated me. I was excited about going to a foreign country and anticipated this new experience. At the same time, stepping out on my own was frightening. The Lord was pushing the limits with me—again.

A lot of *what ifs* went through my mind. "What if God doesn't show up? What if they are not receptive to what I am teaching?" The pastor and his congregation had never been exposed to the ministry of spiritual discernment. The only thing I knew with certainty was that the Lord wanted me to minister in Switzerland. Teaching alone for the first time stretched my faith and trust in God since I had no one else to lean on but Him. I think of how far the Lord has brought me, and I am astounded.

From this experience and many others I have been through, I learned that God is faithful. I have learned that I can do it on my own. "I can do all things through Christ who strengthens me" (Philippians 4:13).

In the past, everything I did was fear based and shame based. I saw myself as a frightened little puppy. Fear and shame had so debilitated me into a state of paralysis, and sometimes I would have anxiety attacks. I would freak out. One day at work, the stapler ran out of staples. I went to a co-worker, grabbed her by the arm, and vigorously shook her and said, "Oh my goodness, the stapler is out of staples."

She did not laugh at me or put me down, but calmly put more staples in the stapler. I am so grateful to her for not scolding me, reprimanding me, or mocking and belittling me, which would have been a perfectly understandable reaction. My behavior to the empty stapler was irrational and embarrassing. Fear had caused me to amplify problems or situations to gigantic proportions. My reactions would be over the top. Constant dread and worry and perceived problems escalated my emotions to anger and panic. Everyday living was trying to cope and to survive. On top of that, I did not want anyone to know about my internal battles since I had no words or understanding for them. I put on a facade the best I could, but life was just hard.

Often, I would blank out or zone out for no reason at all. It might have lasted only a moment or so, but I was aware that I had lost time somehow. Especially while listening to a conversation. All of a sudden, I would lose the whole gist of the conversation or completely forget where I was in the midst of a sentence. When asked what was wrong, my excuse would be that I was daydreaming or that my mind wandered off somewhere, since I had no logical answer.

During the early stages of my healing journey, the Lord wanted me to share my testimony at a Women's Aglow meeting. My main concern was that my mind would blank out and I would not remember where I left off while sharing God's work in my life. So I asked some friends to pray for me specifically for this issue, and the Lord healed me that day. Thank you, Lord.

CHAPTER ONE

GOLD!

As a first generation Chinese Canadian, to tell my difficult story of silent abuse, I need to briefly share a bit of the history of China and how my ancestors made their way to North America. History and culture play a larger part of our lives than we realize, but my story is more about His story—God's story of unconditional love, mercy, and grace.

The discovery of gold in California in 1848 changed the world at the time, and the world has never been the same since. About ten years later, more gold was discovered, this time in Canada, in the province of British Columbia. Men from all over the world, including China, came to prospect for gold in hopes of finding their fortunes. This era of course is known as the Gold Rush. The Chinese coined the name "Gold Mountain" (Gum Saan) when referring to North America. The Gold Rush gave birth to the name Gold Mountain (or Golden Mountain) because of the myth that circulated in China that gold flowed in the streets of Gum Saan. The Chinese believed that upon arrival, gold could literally be picked off the streets. This name has stuck to this present day.

China had a long history of civil wars, famine, and social and political unrest. Heavy taxation along with cruel landlords and warlords were facts of life for decades, and maybe centuries. Millions of people, young and old, were dying of starvation or related diseases, and they were left to die on the streets. These factors motivated my paternal grandfather and thousands of Chinese men to exit their homeland—leaving behind their wives and children to seek a better life for themselves and their families. They took nothing but their cultural and traditional virtue of filial piety. Part of the virtue of filial piety that they held onto was the unquestionable honoring, respecting, and obeying of parents, elders, and those in authority. Fierce pride, an impeccable reputation, and to be held in high esteem are also part of this cultural and traditional virtue of filial piety.

What better place to go than Gum Saan where they could pick up gold off the streets. What they found was something vastly different than what they expected. While many viewed the thousands of Chinese as "coming" to America, to view it more accurately, it should be said that thousands of Chinese were "escaping" to America.

In their search for financial prosperity, they encountered severe persecutions by the non-Asians (also known as Lo Fan). Because the Chinese did not want to antagonize the Lo Fan, they decided not to compete, so most would rework the sites already mined and left behind by the Lo Fan. With their chances diminished of finding gold, few were successful in uncovering the precious metal. Eventually the gold rush subsided, and the Chinese found work in lumber camps, in mining towns, in farms, and in the building of railroads. Their job selections were restricted because of racial discrimination.

In the 1860s a railway was needed to link the East Coast with California. Likewise in Canada, about twenty years later a railway was needed to connect British Columbia in western Canada with eastern Canada. In both cases, there was a massive need of cheap laborers. The Chinese fit the bill. They were hard workers and were willing to work for as little as one dollar a day, whereas the Lo Fan were paid around two fifty to three dollars daily. Consequently, Chinese men were recruited by the thousands. The majority came from the rural area of the province of Kwangtung. When the railway was completed, most chose to stay in Gum Saan rather than return to their homeland, though many still kept the vision of someday returning to their villages to be reunited with their families.

Hard labor, poor living conditions, racial discrimination, language and cultural barriers, and endless challenges from all fronts seemed better than facing life in impoverished China, void of any hope. The men perceived Gum Saan as the land of golden, unlimited opportunities in spite of the injustices they dealt with on a daily basis. Even if they wanted to go back, the fare would have been more than a month's wages in the late 1880s.

Gum Saan represented hope—one element that keeps human beings going, like a fire that burns constantly within us to propel us toward a better tomorrow. To be able to send money back to their loved ones made a life-or-death difference. One dollar bought fifty-five pounds of rice, which could sustain a family for months. The desire to push past the limitations placed upon them caused Chinese men to be more determined than ever. Restaurants, hand-wash laundries, and fruit and vegetable markets appeared and flourished, which in turn provided work for their fellow countrymen.

Chinese women, on the other hand, stayed behind. The Canadian government had banned women from entering into Canada for fear that the Chinese population would grow.

Even without the ban, the women could not accompany their husbands to the land of opportunity because of the inadequate living conditions—nothing but shacks or tents, hardly places for women and children.

Along with their racial prejudice, the Lo Fan feared they would lose their jobs to the Chinese since Asian laborers worked for less money. Responding to public outcry and fears, in 1882 the United States passed The Chinese Exclusion Act, banning any further Chinese immigrants from entering the country. In 1885 the Canadian government placed heavy restrictions in the form of a head tax to stop the influx of Chinese men. When the fifty-dollar head tax did not deter the men, it was raised to one hundred dollars and later to five hundred dollars—equivalent to ten thousand dollars today. The Canadian Government amassed millions of dollars of head tax from the Chinese people who dared to venture out to an unknown world driven by desperation.

In 1923 Canada followed suit with the American government and enacted an outright ban on Chinese immigration, the only legislation designed for a specific ethnic group. If the men returned to China, they might not be allowed to return to Gum Saan, the only hope for their families' survival.

In 1949 the Communists took over China, which changed the future of not only the nation but also the family unit. The Communists sealed the borders shut, which cut off communication with loved ones. The families left behind were now lost. There was nothing to go back to, although a few families managed to escape to Hong Kong, which was a British colony.

The men were permanently separated from their wives and families, resulting in many married men who were forced to live out their days as bachelors.

Unknowingly, the early Chinese immigrant pioneers paved the way for future generations. As with all pioneers, no matter the nationality, they came with their dreams and their courage, determination, and tenacity to succeed.

True, not everyone proved successful in the search for gold. And the price they paid could not be calculated in dollars.

Their payment enabled my father, who came to Canada in the early nineteen hundreds, to carve a successful life for himself and eventually for his family without having to face the same ordeals as his predecessors. My father was among the fortunate ones who found his gold mine, but because of his fierce pride, he lost his daughter who adored him.

My grandfather's first wife died in China, leaving him with a daughter and a son. He remarried, and his second wife bore him two sons; the youngest would eventually be my father. My grandfather worked in San Francisco for a few years, but American food did not agree with his stomach, causing him to struggle with digestive problems. He decided to return to China, but he wanted his sons to take advantage of the available opportunities in North America. He saved enough money to finance his two oldest boys' month-long trip across the Pacific Ocean. They settled in Canada instead of America because the American borders were now closed to all Chinese people. Upon hearing that his older brothers did not fare well either, because of health-related issues, my father asked his dad to send him to Canada. Grandfather didn't have enough money to pay his way.

He asked if the villagers could lend him money to send his last remaining son to Canada. My father was the youngest and the most favored. He never had to do any farm work. He was privileged with a higher education at a time when most people were illiterate. As the scholar in the family, he loved to learn and to read. The villagers scoffed at the idea of sending my father to Canada, mockingly saying my dad's nose was always in the books, and he knew nothing about hard work. Finally, a man in the village had enough faith in my father to lend Grandfather the money. With excitement and anticipation, my father sailed across the ocean to Gum Saan.

CHAPTER TWO

FAMILY LIFE

My father, Bak Fook Art (Bak, which means white, is our surname. Surnames are always placed before our given names) was born in 1884 in the village of Fookwah, in the Toysan district of the province of Kwangtung. He started his adventure at eighteen years old, and with no knowledge of the English or French language, he settled in the French-speaking city of Montreal in the province of Quebec. He took on an Anglicized name: Charles Peck. Growing up, I heard most people called him Charlie, or affectionately, Boss.

My father spent his first few years in Canada with his own hand-wash laundry business. Back then all the laundry was washed in large vats of soap and water using a long wooden rod to stir and pound on the wet, soapy clothes. In two years, he paid back the loan his father owed to send him to Canada. Eventually, he saved enough money to start his own restaurant business. He succeeded from the beginning in this venture with the help of his two brothers, whom I never met. His two cousins—I always addressed them as Asook (Uncle Fred) and Yongsook (Uncle David)—came to help my father at his request. Emigrating from the same village as my father, they arrived as young teenagers in a foreign land and became the cooks in the restaurant. They learned to cook through English cookbooks and had an interpreter translate the recipes for them. Through many trials and errors, they eventually became quite proficient in the Canadian-style cuisine. The restaurants owned by Chinese families at that time did not serve Chinese food yet. (I am told that soldiers coming back to North America after World War II were instrumental in introducing people to Chinese food.)

After a few years of financial success in the restaurant business, my father helped his two brothers return home to China. Their health issues prevented them from being able to endure the hardships of restaurant business, which meant physical labor seven days a week, twelve hours or more a day. He sent them back with enough money so they would not appear as failures and lose face with the villagers.

Canada was my father's gold mine. He had firmly established himself as a successful businessman in Montreal. He faithfully supported his parents and siblings financially until they lost contact with each other when the Communist regime came into power.

Wanting to start a family, he went back to his village to enter into a customary arranged marriage. Many Chinese men did this in spite of the fact that Gum Saan's borders were closed to the Chinese, especially the Chinese women. According to the culture at that time, being unmarried brought on a stigma of shame and dishonor. But my father's marriage was short lived. While he was back in Montreal taking care of his business, his wife died in China from jaundice. Years later, he decided to marry again. He heard of an eligible, young Chinese girl living in British Columbia.

FORCED MARRIAGE

My mother, Seto Wai Gan, was fifteen years old. My father's relatives admonished him that she was too young for him. How different our lives would have turned out had he listened to wise counsel. Refusing to listen to reason, he approached her mother with his proposal for marriage. She consented immediately without giving my mother any options.

Marrying off her daughter would relieve her of the worrisome burden of having to provide for her.

Grandmother had been widowed a few years prior and struggled to make ends meet. She sold leftover flowers from the flower shop at street corners and was nicknamed "the flower lady."

Wai Gan did not want to get married, not to this stranger or to anyone else. She wanted to enjoy her life; after all, she was just a young teenage girl. He was twenty-one years her senior—thirty-six years old. She had no choice but to marry him. Her fate had been decided for her and consequently, so was mine. She wanted to run away, but to where? Our virtue of filial piety dictates absolute obedience to our parents. In despair, the night before her wedding, she contemplated suicide. She was trapped and mortified at the prospect of marrying an "old man" more than twice her age. Emotionally, she never overcame the trauma of the forced marriage. Bitterness, anger, and resentment took root, and my life would be the fruit.

Right after they were married, Wai Gan moved from the West Coast—about four thousand miles—to the eastern part of Canada, where she heard the French language being spoken for the first time. Fortunately, most people spoke broken English. At my father's suggestion, she took on the Anglicized name of Kathleen. She gave birth to my sister Sucainna a year after they married. She did not know what to do with a baby, or even how to care for her child, so her mother moved in with them to help her. She remained with my parents, as each child came along almost yearly.

One year after Sucainna's birth, my mother gave birth to a son, Hubert, followed by another girl, Irene, and two more sons, Raymond and William (Billy). My poor mother, who was barely able to take care of herself, now found herself with five children.

Ironically, as an adult, I found myself in the same situation—five children under my care and not having a clue what to do with them or with myself.

Hubert died around the age of six of a childhood disease. The loss devastated my parents. Hubert was dearly loved, being the "number one son born in Canada," which meant so much, especially to my father. Hubert was their Canadian pride and joy.

Hubert's death nearly took Raymond's life too. One night, shortly after Hubert's death, Raymond was awakened by what appeared to be something like a ball; it came into the room and hovered over him. Out of this ball-like object came a voice, and it sounded like Hubert's voice saying, "It's so peaceful where I am. Come with me. It is beautiful here."

The ball moved toward the window, drawing Raymond with it as if he was in a hypnotic state. This circular object floated through the opened window, and Raymond, having no control, was climbing onto the window ledge. My grandmother happened to walk into the room, and she grabbed Raymond by his pajamas as he was about to fall over the ledge onto the ground from the third floor. She saved his life. When she grabbed him, it was like the "spell" had been broken.

I'M HERE!

By all accounts, it was a happy day when I was born on July 17, 1937. According to my mother, the French waitresses took me from her arms as soon as she came home from the hospital, and they paraded me around my parents' restaurant. They showed me off to all the customers. I was welcomed into the world, and excitement and joy spread all over the restaurant. My parents did not understand the French language, but there was no denying the people's love and enthusiasm for this newborn child. A newborn baby is always a symbol of hope for the future and represents new life and innocence, especially during times of depression and uncertainty.

Halfway around the world, somewhere in China, were my brothers and sisters. Four years before I was born, my parents and grandmother took my siblings—Sucainna, eleven; Irene, nine; Raymond, seven; and Billy, three—to my father's village. My father wanted them to have the best education, which he believed would have been in China where they could be educated according to Chinese tradition and raised in the Chinese culture. My father built a house for them and stayed long enough to help them settle in before returning to Canada with my mother. My siblings were entrusted to the care of my grandmother and my father's family, including aunts and uncles.

The Japanese and the Chinese had a long history of wars with each other, but it was in 1937 that Japan officially declared war on China. Hearing the rumors of impending war, my father made two unsuccessful attempts to find his children and his mother-in-law to bring them back to Canada. Unfortunately, they had already fled their home, and he searched in vain. He had been warned not to attempt a third time.

Devastated and believing that their children would not survive the war, they decided to have another child.

That was how I came to be.

I later found out my siblings survived. But at the time of my joyful birth, my siblings were in the throes of war. While waitresses paraded me around with joy and laughter, they faced starvation and death. I lived in security and never had to experience hunger. They lived with the uncertainty of whether they would make it through the day.

My earliest memory is of my mother cooking meals for me. I lived alone with her in Montreal's Chinatown, and the place was dark and spooky, with mice always scurrying around the floors.

We lived apart from my father, as he was busy establishing a restaurant that he recently took over in another part of the city. If this venture proved viable, we would then join him. Overwhelming success came almost immediately. By the time I was born, my father had already bought and sold a nightclub and five restaurants in succession. This new restaurant was named The New Dainty Cafe—it was his gold mine.

In the 1920s he rented a three-story building. He made the first floor into a restaurant and the second floor into a nightclub. The third floor was for the family, where my parents, siblings (before leaving for China), and uncles lived. The nightclub was short lived because of the many drunken brawls that took place at night. The police were constantly called to bring order. My father closed the nightclub and decided to focus his attention solely on the restaurant instead. During this time my father became friends with a policeman who later became the chief of police. Years later, this policeman would be instrumental in helping my dad in a challenging situation.

I was five years old when we moved from the dark and spooky place to another dark and spooky place to join my father to live at 200 Atwater Street, across from the Atwater Market. My father had bought the restaurant knowing the area had problems with hoodlums and troublemakers. They hung in gangs around the restaurant, which kept the legitimate customers away. My father called the police and the chief of police came and was surprised that the owner of the restaurant was my dad. Dad was also surprised the chief of police was the same policeman he had befriended years ago. The chief warned the troublemakers—my father was a personal friend of his and they had better leave him and his restaurant alone. Problem solved. They never came back.

Next to the restaurant was a stable for the horses used for delivering milk, bread, blocks of ice for iceboxes, and other necessities. Many times I watched the horses being re-shoed. Beside the stable were two gigantic, two-story-high ice makers. This ice was shaped in blocks, ready to be delivered to homes with iceboxes. I would crawl through a small opening into the cold rooms to cool off in the hot, muggy summer days. Air conditioners at the time were only for the wealthy.

Across from us stood a huge lumberyard and lumber mill. Up the street were two taverns, one on each side of the street, and further up was a scrap metal yard. Our restaurant was on the corner, and up the street at the other corner was another Chinese-owned restaurant, also a gold mine because of the ideal location. The Atwater Market was a farmers' market. The stores in the market sold fresh fruits and vegetables, freshly butchered and cut meats, freshly killed and plucked poultry, fresh fish, and many other items that would now be labeled as organic. The New Dainty Cafe, the Atwater Market, and the street we lived on teemed with a variety of people.

There were the men from the lumberyard, truck drivers, garbage collectors, men who delivered fresh bread and milk, shoppers and soldiers, and tanks and armored trucks were on parade daily. WWII was still on, but I had no comprehension of what wartime meant.

Watching the diversity of people come and go from the restaurant kept me busy, and the weekends were the most exciting for me. The farmers arrived early Saturday morning before the sun came out with their trucks loaded with their goods. Their products ranged from fruits and vegetables, flowers, fresh maple syrup, and fresh honey to live chickens and huge carcasses of beef and pork. I'd wake up early in the morning and watch the caravan of trucks arrive. After the farmers finished unloading their trucks and setting up their stalls, they would come into our restaurant for a ten-cent breakfast of coffee and toast served with strawberry jam or marmalade. My Uncle Fred sliced about thirty loaves of bread by hand ahead of time and placed the slices on the oven range. I helped by buttering the toast. Uncle Fred complained that I used too much butter. The farmers, though, complained that Uncle Fred used too little butter.

I watched as farmers arranged their beautiful array of flowers. Often, they would give me a bleeding heart flowering plant. I wonder now if that was a prophetic picture of my heart, because the times I received flowers from the farmers, it would always be a bleeding heart plant.

The farmers picked up and left Saturday evenings, leaving behind garbage strewn all over the marketplace. So Sundays meant clean up time for the city workers. Although our family was considered well off, I was aware of poverty. Saturday evenings and Sunday mornings, many young children and some adults would search through the garbage left behind by the farmers. They picked up rotten fruits and vegetables, discarded lettuce, and wilted cabbage leaves.

During World War II, people lived on ration stamps, which meant that the purchase of butter, sugar, coffee, meat, and other staples were limited. These restrictions were necessary because not only was there a shortage of food, but food was needed to feed the military who were fighting overseas. I saw the strain on many people's faces as they struggled to survive and to make ends meet. Their anxiety served as a constant reminder not to take food for granted. When my dad raised the price of an ice cream cone to six cents from five cents, there were so many complaints that he lowered it back to five cents. A penny meant a lot during those lean years. There was never a shortage of food for us as a family or for the waitresses who worked for my parents.

I enjoyed the activity of the Atwater Market—the busyness of the restaurant and being in the midst of the hustle and bustle of my surroundings.

But most of all, I loved spending time with Dad and Uncle Fred. Helping in the kitchen was always fun, though I was more of a hindrance than a helper. My dad was frugal and used his money for investments as well as sending money back home to his parents, his siblings, and my siblings, whom I had yet to meet. Not having toys to play with did not bother me. Toys were considered frivolous and a waste of money to my parents. My dad had a goal. Until now, he had always rented the business premises and our living quarters, but he wanted to own his own property. We all lived a frugal life so he could fulfill his dream. At the same time, he showed generosity to those in need.

Living frugally was a common thread among immigrants, no matter their homeland. They worked long hours and rarely bought anything outside of necessities. They were accustomed to living with so little that many were able to fulfill their monetary goals. Christmas, birthdays, Easter, or other special occasions were never celebrated in my home. Coming from China, I imagine that these holidays were foreign to my parents and held no significance. Uncle Fred always baked me a special cake for my birthday—the only indication that it was a day to honor my birth. The cake tasted like strawberry shortcake. I felt even more special on the years it had real strawberries on it.

MY MOTHER

My mother hated her physical appearance as well as her circumstances. Short in stature, she only stood about five feet tall, and the weight gained during her pregnancies was never lost. It did not help that she could not buy nice clothes for herself because of her weight. She sewed her own clothes, but they did not compliment her figure. She lived in a constant state of depression and drank a lot of alcohol at a time when it was unheard of for a Chinese woman to imbibe liquor. Not only was it unheard of, but culturally it posed a source of shame for the family. We did not talk about it in the house, and we dared not mention it outside of the home. The entire family turned a blind eye to it, but no one knew what to do since she was not approachable. To my mother, it helped drown the pain, the trauma, and the unhappiness of being married to a man she loathed. She blamed my father for her misery, whether it was legitimately his fault or not. Many times, even when sober, her frustration and anger were released onto others, but in particular, on her children.

My mother mourned the death of her dreams, the sudden death of her carefree teenage years. She cried often, and many times she unloaded her sorrows to me when I was but a young girl. My mother had no one else with whom to share her pain. How could I, as a five-, six-, or seven-year-old, understand her complaints against her husband, the father I dearly loved? How could I make this woman happy? I had no answer. I could only listen. In a childlike way, I saw and felt her pain as she poured out in hopeless despair.

My mother had entered into a forced marriage, and only when as an adult did I come to see that after their marriage, she never matured. It was as if she were still a child, unable to cope with being a wife and mother. Emotionally she refused to find the strength to deal with everyday life. No effort was made to mother me or love me or establish any sort of foundation in my life. At night she looked after the restaurant, which was open twenty-four hours a day, every day.

Her daytime hours were spent mostly in bed.

I did not have the same deep love for her as I did for Dad. She disconnected from her emotions and from life. My mother existed in a world of her own, where no one else was allowed in.

Not having a mother to meet my needs emotionally was frustrating. I remember—I must have been about seven years old—I was pounding on her chest, yelling, "Mom, you don't hear me. You don't understand me. You don't even try!"

As I look back, I clearly see that we never connected heart-to-heart, spirit-to-spirit, or mother-to-daughter. Aside from living with her pain, despair, and alcoholism, I know little about her—if she had any siblings, or what her life was like growing up, or even whether she was born in China or British Columbia.

And I certainly hadn't known as a child how her emotionally crippled life would help derail my life and lead to an emotional train wreck from which I believed I'd never recover.

Even as I write this book, I cannot refer to her as "Mom." She was my mother in that she gave birth to me. But she was not my mom—that relationship between us never took root and therefore never blossomed.

MY FATHER

Dad was the brain behind the restaurant business. During my childhood years, my parents never did any physical work. They mostly sat behind the cash register looking after the money coming in. Dad handled all the finances and the decision making.

Dad was not tall either, but most Chinese people back then were small framed. He always wore old black trousers, held up with his suspenders, and a faded, aged white shirt with his sleeves rolled up. He was about five foot one, quiet in nature, and he enjoyed reading his Chinese newspaper. He wrote many letters to his family back home, sealing the envelope with a special seal with Chinese characters on it—so the recipient would know if the letter had been tampered with.

Dad and I loved each other deeply. I enjoyed seeing his smile and hearing his laughter. My dad was a generous and trusting man with a big heart. During and after the war, Canadians struggled to survive. Many times people would come to the restaurant without any money, asking for something to eat. They never left disappointed, as they were usually given a bowl or two of soup, some bread, and a cup of coffee.

On one occasion, a customer slipped the restaurant silverware into his pocket. When confronted by my father, the customer denied it. Dad persisted. Finally the customer admitted his guilt and slowly took four or five pieces of silverware from his pocket. My dad asked him if he needed the silverware or if he needed money. The man remained silent, with his head downward. Dad, in his broken English said, "Take, take," pointing to the silverware and asking, "What you want? Me help, me help."

The customer was so ashamed that he left the restaurant with his head downcast without the silverware. I thought, Why don't you tell my dad what you want? He will help you. Instead, he did not utter one word. He just left in silence.

One businessman's life turned around because of my father. The butcher was a gambler and an alcoholic and had spent the money that was supposed to pay his suppliers. So as my dad bought his meat from this butcher's store, he was expecting his meat order to arrive. When the order failed to turn up, Dad phoned his meat supplier. The businessman's son answered. A lot of commotion could be heard in the background. Dad asked, "My meat, my meat?"

The son replied, sobbing, "Our father spent all the money, we can't pay our supplier, and we can't get the meat."

Dad walked to the store, which was located in the Atwater Market, handed over five hundred dollars, and said, "Here, you pay," meaning to pay the supplier.

A full-course meal, including soup, dessert, and coffee only cost twenty-five cents. The daily newspaper cost three pennies, so five hundred dollars was a fortune. The businessman was so taken aback by Dad's gesture that he stopped gambling and drinking and put his business back in order.

One of the restaurant's waitresses, whom I'll call Sarah, told me her account of how my father helped her out. Her mother had passed away, and she and her younger sister were left with their irresponsible father. He spent his wages at the taverns and many times did not come home until late at night. The two fended for themselves with barely any food in the house, nor did they have proper clothes or shoes.

One day their father left for work and never came back.

Sarah was about fourteen years old. She knew she had to do something to take care of herself and her sister. Walking around the area, she came upon Dad's restaurant looking for a job. He hired her upon hearing her story, knowing she was underage. Fortunately, she looked like she was sixteen, which was the legal age to work. Before starting to work for him, she asked Dad for some money for food and a much-needed pair of shoes. He gave it to her with no questions asked and not requiring a promissory note. Sarah remained faithful to my dad by working for him for many years, always expressing her deep gratitude toward my father.

Many stories circulated about my father's generosity in contributing to people's successes, or in helping them to overcome their challenges and obstacles. God favored him with financial resources, and he also had favor with people, whether Asian or non-Asian.

Dad was a respected elder of the Chinese community, well known for his success as a restaurateur and a benefactor always willing to help people in need. He was a learned man, well versed in Confucius' teachings, in Chinese history, and the art of Chinese calligraphy. He cared about the community and was opposed to seeing many of the bachelor Chinese men who, because of boredom, spent their free time gambling away their savings. His admonitions fell upon deaf ears.

Many elderly Chinese immigrants—stranded in a foreign country with no hope of reconciling with their families—lived and died in poverty because they could not overcome their gambling addictions.

CHAPTER THREE

FROM THE MOUNTAINTOP TO THE DEEP VALLEY

*S*ome people come to know the Lord and remember the date, place, and even the time. I still remember the exact spot where I was standing. I was six when Dad was getting me ready for bed one evening. He was wiping my face when I asked, "Dad, where did I come from?"

"God created you," he replied.

"Who is God?" I asked.

Dad answered, "God created you. He created the whole world and everything in it."

"Where is God?" I asked.

Dad responded, "He is in heaven. He is everywhere, and He is all around you. He sees everything and knows everything. He sees you right now, and He loves you."

I didn't understand.

I asked, "He sees me right now?"

Dad said, "Yes, God is watching you right this moment."

In that instant, I felt a surge of power, like an explosion hit my chest. It was almost as if something had burst open inside of me. Instantly I knew God. I knew who God was. Every word my dad shared with me was imprinted in my heart permanently, even until this day. I was so excited.

Since then, I have never been the same. God opened my eyes and gave me a gift—the ability to see spiritually. It was as if I saw an extra layer on top of my physical surroundings. I felt, sensed, and literally saw His presence.

To this day, I am still puzzled how my father shared in perfect English about the love and omnipresence of God. He never spoke to me in English, always in Chinese. Whenever he spoke with non-Asians, it was with broken English and a lot of hand gestures. So hearing these perfect English words coming from my father as he shared about the love of God was nothing short of a miracle.

I will never forget the following day. I was barely out the door, about to walk to school, when I looked up at the sky and was amazed at what I saw and felt. I saw the awesome and glorious presence of God. The sight was and still is beyond description. I lowered my gaze—His presence was also there. As my eyes took in my surroundings, I became aware of the omnipresence of God. I felt bathed in His presence.

As a child, I did not have the words to properly explain what I was experiencing. As an adult, I still don't. All I can say is that the Lord touched me. He filled me with such a sense of joy that I started to skip and continued skipping all the way to school. The joy of the Lord remained within me throughout my childhood.

The Lord knew I would need this joy to sustain me for what was to come. I believe the outpouring of this same joy caused my siblings, whom I would meet a couple of years later, to resent me. They couldn't understand why I was constantly happy, and for reasons unknown, it annoyed them.

I'M NOT WHITE?

I was in first grade when some of my classmates invited me to go with them after school to a place with toys and games for kids. I tagged along, and as we stood in front of the building, I noticed a sign: Community Centre. Kids were allowed once a week after school to play there for a couple of hours. The thought of being able to play with games and toys excited me as I walked up the flight of stairs. As soon as we reached the doorway, my friends ran in. However, when I followed, a lady stopped me from entering.

She said, "You can't come in."

I asked why, and she said I needed ten cents to get in. I did not have ten cents, nor did I recall seeing my friends give anything to the lady. They just ran in. I left there knowing my dad would give me the ten cents I needed. The following week, with ten cents in my hand, I confidently went again. I was denied entrance.

I said, "But I have the ten cents to get in."

She said, "You still can't come in."

"Why not?" I asked.

She gave me a look of disdain. "Because this place is for white people, and you are not white."

Puzzled, I went home to my dad and asked, "What do I have to do to be white?"

He said, "Drink lots of milk." So I did. I drank lots and lots of milk. (Being lactose intolerant explains the many tummy aches I suffered as a child.) I checked the mirror often to see if there were any changes to my face. No changes. I still looked the same. I decided to try again. Since I drank a lot of milk, I was hoping that something would change. This time the same lady was insistent and firm. "No, no! You need to understand. You will never be able to come here. You are not white."

Her words puzzled me. I didn't grasp the totality of what she was saying. I had never experienced racism before. All sorts of people came to my family's restaurant, and everyone treated us nicely. Determined to be white, I walked home and found some powder and smeared it on my face. My dad asked me what I was doing with this white powder on my face. I explained that I wanted to go to the Community Centre to play after school but couldn't get in because I wasn't white. Then he explained to me that I was Chinese, and my skin color was different and could not be changed. What a relief! I finally knew why I was not white.

I was Chinese. And I was okay with it. That was the one and only time I experienced racial prejudice while living in Montreal. In truth, it didn't bother me at all.

MY HOME

In our three-bedroom apartment upstairs from the restaurant, we did not have hot water, a shower, a toilet, or a bathtub. I used a little spittoon for a toilet, and my mother emptied it every day. I took baths and washed my hair only once a week, thankfully—always on a Saturday. For this ordeal I had to start the fire in the potbelly stove, fill a bucket with water, and put the bucket of water on the stove to heat up. When it was hot, I emptied the water into a galvanized metal vat just large enough for me to fit in. I heated up five or six buckets of water before there was enough to bathe. Knowing I would have to empty it, I never filled up the vat too much. Mice and cockroaches jumped out everywhere. At that time, there wasn't a code or standard of living, but if there was, our living conditions would definitely not have been acceptable.

The building had been rundown and neglected for many years. The plastered walls were cracked and exposed behind the chipped paint. The worn linoleum revealed planks of rotting wood flooring. The damp, moldy, and rusted counter area around the sink was unsanitary and sorely in need of repair. We lived there for almost seven years and had to move because the city condemned it, and the building was to be torn down. My mother never cleaned or dusted, so dust balls floated all over the place. A potbelly stove heated our living area. I was proud of myself for being able to get the fire going during the extremely cold winters, sometimes taking several attempts.

In spite of all this, I was a happy and content child.

While our apartment was shabby and dirty, the restaurant downstairs stayed in tip-top shape. The tables, chairs, booths, and floors were built with planks of wood and coated with brown paint. The eight circular tables varied in size, each seating anywhere from four to six people. There were two counters with about nine stools in total. I mostly sat at the counter, close to my dad, sitting on the stool by the window and looking out onto the marketplace. The restaurant easily sat eighty-five people, and during lunchtime, people stood in line waiting for an empty seat.

MY JOURNEY DOWNHILL

My world evolved around my dad. I loved him immensely. We hung out together, talked, went for walks, or simply enjoyed each other's presence.

One particular school day, I came downstairs, and as usual, I walked through the restaurant on my way out the door to head off for school. A customer sat at one of the tables, and my dad was at a distance behind the counter by the cash register. I said bye to *baba* (Chinese for daddy) as was my custom, and as I waved my hand on my way out the door, the customer said to me, "Aren't you going to kiss your daddy good-bye?"

I stopped and wondered what that was all about. He continued, "Kiss your daddy good-bye."

Kissing and hugging was not, and still is not, part of the Chinese culture. It was something I had not experienced or seen. I knew my dad loved me just by looking in his eyes. His eyes and smile conveyed the love in his heart for me. The man insisted again and said, "Come and kiss your daddy good-bye."

Oriental parents demonstrate their affections toward their children by their actions and deeds rather than outward displays of affection. I was never hugged or kissed, and the words "I love you" were never spoken in English or Chinese to me. Such displays were foreign to my parents also. The customer's words bewildered me. I had no idea what to do or how to respond.

So the easiest thing for me was to go out the door and continue on to school.

When I came home from school and greeted my father as usual with "baba, baba," he did not talk to me. Not knowing something was wrong, I continued to chatter away.

He turned and walked away from me.

He never smiled at me again.

He never talked to me again.

Ever.

I literally lost my father that day. I had a dad and a mom, but I was orphaned, and I was only six years old.

To make matters worse, I did not have any clue as to what I did wrong. Or why my dad turned away from me in silence.

This event was not only traumatic, but it altered the course of my life and my future.

I did not cry. I was not aware of feeling pain. I went from having this amazing experience with God to having the most important person in my life stolen from me. I was alone and lost in my own home. As a child, I had no concept about Chinese culture or traditional filial piety or *mow min*—no face, losing face. Chinese tradition considers losing face akin to losing dignity, honor, and respect, and it is an unforgiveable offense.

I had caused my father to lose face.

FAMILY DYNAMICS

Life abruptly changed. I had no one to turn to, no one I could talk to, no one to laugh with, and no one to make me smile. My father had been that person for me.

(Psalm 27:10: "When my father and my mother forsake me, Then the Lord will take care of me." I didn't know this verse at the time, but later in my life, God revealed Himself to me as my heavenly Father who never turned His back on me.)

I rarely saw my mother sober. But I did get beatings from her with a strap in her drunken rages. She used a thick leather strap that my father sharpened his razor on. The first time she chased me with that strap, I ran downstairs to my dad, frightened.

"Baba! Baba! Mom wants to beat me. She is drunk!"

He turned and walked away.

Painfully, I stepped back upstairs, so disappointed and discouraged that he would not help me. My mother grabbed me and threw me onto the bed as I was screaming, frightened and terrified. She pulled my pants down.

"I wish you were dead. I wish you'd never been born!" Why was she screaming hateful words at me? Why did she wish me dead?

It didn't make any sense. I hadn't done anything wrong.

My hands grabbed onto the rails of the bed as I braced myself for pain. When the strap hit me, it did not hurt. I felt no pain. I thought, This is not going to be as bad as I thought it would be. I started to relax and just allowed her to vent her anger until she decided to stop.

Whether it was the voice of an angel or the voice of God, I do not know, but I heard a voice clearly say to me, "Scream. Scream as loud as you can, because she will hit you harder if you don't." So I screamed as loud as I could.

When she finished, I fell fast asleep. My first thought upon waking was, it was a bad dream. The beating never really happened because I didn't feel any pain. But the red marks on my skin showed that it did happen. God, in His mercy, took the pain for me. I don't know how else to explain it, but I never once experienced physical pain any time I was beaten.

The emotional pain would prove far more painful, as I would find out in my adult years.

My mother at one point marveled that I was still able to sit after she had whipped me so hard with the strap. It bothered her that she couldn't crush my happiness. She remarked in a tone of resentment on a few occasions, "Why are you always so happy?"

I shrugged my shoulders because I did not know how to answer her. I realize now that it was the joy of the Lord.

Another time, my mother wanted to cut my hair. She was drunk again, and I was terrified as she chased me with the sharp pointed scissors in her hand. I ran to my dad for help because, I thought, surely he would help me this time. How could he possibly refuse me? This was serious. I was convinced she was going to stab me.

My dad refused to help me.

I was stunned. I begged him to rescue me from my mother, but he ignored me. After several rejected attempts of pleading with him for help, I never approached my dad again.

It was a moment of profound pain—the horrible realization that my dad would never be my protector again, even in the face of great danger. I was no longer his little girl.

I no longer had a father.

So I resigned myself to letting my mother cut my hair. She didn't stab me, but my hair turned out choppy and uneven, of course. I was so embarrassed to face my classmates with such a ridiculous haircut. The many haircuts finally stopped when I found the clippers and secretly removed the screw that held them together.

Growing up in a house with a violent, angry mother, whether drunk or sober, brought instability, fear, and confusion into my life. In the mornings around seven thirty as I would get ready for school, my mother would terrorize me. She would emerge stumbling from her bedroom, still drunk or hung over from the night before, with disheveled hair and an angry face, making incomprehensible sounds with her voice. My heart would skip a beat as she came close to me. Was she going to yell at me? Was she going to hit me? I never knew what to expect.

Some mornings I would find her passed out on the floor. Unable to bring her back to consciousness left me feeling she was dead.

Other times, she would trash a room by throwing everything on the floor: clothes, books, lamps, everything and anything she could grab hold of.

On my seventh birthday, the waitresses and some of the customers held a surprise birthday party for me—my first and only birthday party. They surprised me with presents, and I had a store-bought birthday cake too. I felt so special. "Happy Birthday Mimi" was even written on the cake. There were enough presents to fill a table and a half: dolls, a high chair for the dolls, a child-sized table and chair set, a tea set, a blackboard, coloring books, crayons, and so much more. With excitement and enthusiasm, I gathered them all, took them upstairs to my room, and placed them neatly in my bedroom and on my shelf. I reveled in the fact that I had toys of my own for the very first time.

Shortly after, when my mother was in one of her angry moods again, she chopped up every one of my brand new gifts and burnt them in the potbelly stove. I managed to salvage only one doll. I saw her take an axe to the toys that meant so much to me.

I cried, "Mom, what are you doing?"

She replied, "It's useless, a waste. What do you need them for anyway?"

I walked away bewildered and extremely hurt. When my toys "died" in the raging fire from the potbelly stove, it was as though a part of me also died. Why would my mother want to hurt me so much? Her cruelty was beyond my understanding.

During the Christmas season when I was in the second grade, our class had a beautifully decorated tall Christmas tree. A few days before our holiday break, the teacher asked if anyone who did not have a Christmas tree would want to take that one. I quickly shot up my hand. We had never had a Christmas tree, and I wanted it bad.

On the last day of school for the Christmas break, my teacher asked me who was going to come pick up the tree. I told her no one was coming and that I could take the tree home by myself. By her look, I could tell she was surprised, but she also saw the look of determination in my little face and wished me good luck and Merry Christmas. I was embarrassed that my parents weren't coming to help, but I had not mentioned the tree to them.

My parents never came to see me sing or perform at any of the school functions. I knew they wouldn't come for a tree. (School functions were a mix of joy and sadness. I loved to perform, but I could see all the other parents except for mine.)

Being a tiny second grader, I managed to haul that big tree by its trunk through thick snow and ice for an entire mile. I had to stop several times to catch my breath, but I was determined. While hauling the tree, I kept visualizing pretty ornaments and streamers around it. In my mind, I was decorating the tree and didn't feel the bitter cold. I was just happy to have a real Christmas tree. It didn't matter how long it took me to get it home or how cold it was outside.

In my innocence and naivety, I assumed my parents would love the tree as much as I did. How could they not?

With a sense of accomplishment and pride, I hauled it into the restaurant. I still remember my parents' stern faces.

"What are you doing with that?" my mother demanded.

"My teacher gave it to us. Isn't that nice?" I said, trying to sell it to them as best I could. "Look at how pretty it is. I can't wait to decorate it."

It was near Christmastime, and while everyone else in the western world was feeling cheerful, my mother was in her same mood: bad and mean. "Get rid of it. Throw it in the garbage!" she yelled.

There were customers in the restaurant, and we were speaking in Chinese, but I knew they could tell what was transpiring. A sense of embarrassment flooded me, and I lowered my voice and enthusiasm.

"Please, Mom, let me keep it. I promise I'll take care of it. You don't have to do anything. I'll decorate it and do all the cleanup. I promise." I pleaded.

Her face didn't change.

"I don't even have to decorate it, so you don't have to buy any decorations." I just wanted the tree. I could imagine the decorations on it. I would pretend it looked the way it did in the classroom.

"I said get rid of it!" My mother yelled, causing everyone in the restaurant—the waitresses that I knew well, and the customers—to stare at me. My little heart crushed, I hauled the tree to the garbage. I visited the leaning tree many times. I could envision it standing straight and tall with the beautiful decorations, until the fateful day came when it was hauled away in the garbage truck.

My mother was so unhappy that she was never hospitable to some of the Chinese visitors we had. She was downright mean. One man who came by occasionally was nicknamed "Pig Farmer" because he went to all the Chinese restaurants selling pigs' feet, pigs' skins, and other edibles that only Chinese people would eat. I felt so sorry for him because my mother treated him with disrespect and disdain. He impressed me because I saw how hard he worked, and yet he was always jovial. He was a soft-spoken man and seemed to have a kind personality. Short in build, his back was hunched over from the strain of having to pull his heavy cart with wooden wheels for miles selling his products. His skin was weathered and brown, and hardship could be seen through his rough, gnarled hands and his wrinkled face. My mother behaved terribly toward him, but my father was always hospitable as they conversed with each other. The man was always given something to eat before he went back on the road. Because he traveled to so many different places, the Pig Farmer would bring news from other Chinese people and from their homeland. He was one of the ways some Chinese stayed connected.

Even though it was never articulated in the house, I knew my mother's alcoholism and nastiness was a family shame and embarrassment. Not only that, I also knew to keep it a secret. My mother's behavior was highly unusual for an oriental woman. The Chinese community was small and tight-knit. Everyone knew about each other's personal and not-so-personal affairs, and any news, whether good or bad, traveled fast. If the community knew about my mother's alcoholism, it was never spread around or gossiped—most likely out of respect for my father. (I discovered this later when I moved to Toronto. The Chinese community there heard of my father and his good reputation, but no one knew about my mother's behavior, for which I was grateful. I did not want that stigma of shame to fall on me, causing me to lose face.) I became aware of the importance of having an untarnished reputation, of having pride in ourselves as well as our parents and our ancestral lineage, all part of our traditional filial piety.

But it is the same filial piety that sent me on a downward slide faster than a sled on ice.

MY DEAR UNCLE FRED (ASOOK)

I was eight years old when I was almost kidnapped from our backyard one day, and it was Uncle Fred who rescued me. Behind the restaurant was a very small backyard, a little bigger than the size of an average bedroom. The backyard was used as a passageway to go to the back door of the kitchen of the restaurant, where most of the deliveries of restaurant supplies were made. Uncle Fred's warning of the rats that frequented the backyard was enough to keep me from lingering there. The backyard was loosely fenced with old, thin wooden slats. The entrance had an old wooden gate that could be easily opened or closed, making easy access for the delivery of supplies. I happened to be in the backyard when a man came in and abruptly picked me up. As he was pulling me away, I grabbed onto the old wobbly wooden post of the gate to the yard. He had me under his one arm and with his free hand, he was trying to pry my grip loose from the post. The kitchen being next to the yard, I knew my uncle was there, and I screamed as loud as I could, "Asook, Asook." After much yelling and screaming for my uncle to help me, he finally heard me and chased the man away with a cleaver. I remember thinking how grateful I was for my uncle. I knew that my father would have ignored my cries.

After my father installed his wall of silence and my mother started bullying me, my affections transferred to my Uncle Fred. I grew to love him, and he was someone I could turn to, though I only saw him when I went into the kitchen during the daytime. Sometimes I would spend time with him as he peeled potatoes or when he peeled the apples for pies. Seldom did he have a spare moment. There was always something that needed to get done, but he always welcomed me. In Uncle Fred, I had someone to love and to talk to. But as wonderful as he was, he couldn't make up for my father's rejection. Just as my love for him couldn't make up for his heartbreak.

As previously mentioned, Uncle Fred's dad was my paternal grandfather's younger brother, and he immigrated to Canada as a teenager to work in my father's restaurant. After saving enough money, Uncle Fred went back to China to an arranged marriage. He came back to Canada, leaving his young bride behind (as was typical back then). Uncle Fred's goal was to become financially stable and eventually return to China to live. A short time later, Uncle Fred received the news that his wife had been raped and murdered in China.

He dutifully took it upon himself to avenge his wife's tragic death. He sailed across the Pacific Ocean back to his village. He chased down the culprit and avenged his wife's death by murdering the man rather than having him arrested to stand trial. He then proceeded to the police station, confessed his crime, and served six months in jail. It was a sort of token penalty, since avenging his wife's death was an act of honor, which was acceptable during that period of time—the 1920s or 1930s. He came back to Canada after serving his time in prison. He did what was required to save face, that is, his dignity, honor, self-respect remained intact.

As he recounted his story to me, he shared that he had lost his reason to live. His hopes and dreams died with his wife. He never remarried. He carried a weight of sadness about him.

At the restaurant, we didn't have dishwashers, so my uncles, who did all the cooking, washed the dishes, pots, and pans by hand. Uncle Fred worked the day shift by himself and Uncle David worked the night shift by himself. Together, but working apart, they kept everything running smoothly in the kitchen. Uncle Fred ordered supplies in his broken English, and the French-speaking suppliers responded in their broken English.

Uncle Fred always fixed my breakfast and lunch, and I ate it in the kitchen. Breakfast was usually porridge or eggs or pancakes. Lunch was whatever was ready made in the kitchen. Since lunchtime was a very busy time for him, he would give me a bowl of soup or stew or mashed potatoes and gravy, or yummy shepherd's pie, all things I still love to this present day. I ate with my parents at dinnertime in the dining room of the restaurant, and that was the only time we ate Chinese food, which was also prepared by my Uncle Fred.

Sometimes I was not allowed to eat supper because of something I did or did not do. But because my father refused to speak to me, it was always a mystery as to the reason for the punishment.

But I knew Uncle Fred would not let me go hungry. I would sneak into the kitchen through the back door and hide underneath the long kitchen worktable, crouching down in between huge kitchen pots.

Uncle Fred dropped food down to me as he prepared the meals. My father caught him once and reprimanded him for feeding me behind his back. My uncle later told me he was not happy with the way my parents treated me. Because of the traditional filial piety, he was not in any position to help me since he was younger than my father, and he had been warned not to meddle with the way I was being raised.

One day, he told my dad to stop treating me so harshly. He said, "Take a good look at her. Can't you see that she has found favor with the gods? You will incur the wrath of the gods for mistreating her."

My father did not take him seriously.

THE FALLOUT: DISSOCIATIVE DISORDER AND PROBLEMS AT SCHOOL

How could I possibly handle the total rejection of my father, who was my world, and the terrors of an alcoholic mother?

Unknowingly, each disappointment, each trauma, and each rejection was causing deep emotional pain that seriously affected my ability to learn, comprehend, and mature emotionally.

Children are not capable of handling excess pain, whether physical, emotional, or psychological.

I locked painful memories away in the back of my mind and developed amnesia. Of course, the pain would surface later. But I survived because of this coping mechanism. Experts today call it dissociative disorder.

Because of my dissociation, my school years were painful and frightening. I was able to hear the teachers' words, but their words had no meaning to me. This applied to my reading also. I read and wrote quite well, but the words and understanding escaped me. My teachers accused me of being rebellious and disobedient, but in reality, their words did not register with me. I was yelled at often, which compounded my fears, causing me to shut down. (To this day, if someone gets angry at me, it has a paralyzing effect, albeit to a lesser degree than when I was a child.)

A gym teacher reprimanded me in anger for something I must have done wrong, but I was not aware of what it was. After her scolding, she said, "Now do you understand?"

I answered, "No, I don't understand."

She continued yelling until I lied and said "Yes, I understand" so she would stop scolding me. Those years were spent in frustration and confusion. My fears escalated when teachers grabbed me by my collar or shook me. I was seen as a "problem child" because I was forever in trouble.

I couldn't focus, my grades dropped from As and Bs in my first two years to Cs and Ds. My fifth and sixth grade teacher was constantly angry with the class, which caused many of us to be afraid of her. After I finished fifth grade, a classmate told me how sorry she felt for me that I had to have the same angry teacher in the sixth grade. I was devastated and wished I could run away and escape my fate. As for my sixth grade and onward school years, I have no recollection—they are all a blur. I eventually graduated with a C minus average.

Fear and trauma caused me to be mentally immobilized so it was difficult to think, retain information, or remember what was being said. I had difficulty thinking logically or rationally or piecing things together in their proper sequences. I was debilitated in decision making. I did not grow up equipped with basic life skills that people take for granted.

Dr. James G. Friesen, in his book *Uncovering the Mystery of MPD* (multiple personality disorder), wrote, "Dissociation is the most wonderful defense God made to help people stay healthy in the face of serious child abuse" (Wipf and Stock, 1997).

Dissociation enables those living through extreme emotional, psychological, or physical abuse to be able to cope and to survive. This is essential for children because they are so vulnerable and are in their formative years.

But the effects of abuse and disassociation will not stay locked away forever.

CHAPTER FOUR

THE END OF A WAR
STARTED A NEW ONE

The war with Germany ended in May 1945, though the war with Japan continued on for a few more months. Still, VE Day—Victory in Europe—was celebrated on May 8, 1945. Surprisingly, my mother took me downtown to be part of the celebrations. I could not believe what I saw—the streets were packed with so many people. They were all laughing, singing, shouting, and dancing. People were hugging, cars were honking, streetcars were clanging their bells, and confetti and newspapers were flying all over the place. I saw a lady joyously fling out her fur coat from the streetcar we were in and watched as people trampled all over it. It was nothing like the somber, serious tone we all lived in—it was as if everyone had gone mad, but in a celebratory way. It was a joyous mayhem that I (and I'm sure millions more) will never forget.

Most of my siblings in China survived the war. My sister Irene, whom I never met, committed suicide at a young age. She was sick with pneumonia and suffered much pain. The war-torn area where they had lived had little food and even less in terms of medical supplies. Sucainna, my oldest sister, later told me of the cruelty that Irene was subjected to from my grandmother. Apparently, my grandmother was not sympathetic to Irene's plight and many times would curse her to die instead of trying to nurse her back to health. Irene was made to feel like a hindrance to the struggling family and attempted to commit suicide twice by drinking lye, a caustic chemical used at that time to make soap. When those attempts failed, she succeeded in ending her short life by hanging herself.

As for my grandmother, when the war was over, she chose to go back to her late husband's village to spend her remaining years there instead of returning to Canada.

She did so in keeping with the Chinese tradition held at that time—that the wife should be buried in her husband's village.

My siblings arrived back in Canada in March of 1946 after thirteen long years away from home. An only child for the first nine years of my life, I had no idea how much my life was about to change, yet remain the same at the same time. It was an extremely cold and bitter winter day—the ground was frozen with thick layers of snow as I walked home from school. The sidewalks were lined with high snow banks that had accumulated after every snowfall. It was so cold that day that the door handle of the entrance to the restaurant was caked with ice, and my mitt stuck to the ice. I struggled to open the door, and finally my mother opened it from the inside.

What first caught my attention was that my mother and my father were both smiling. I rarely saw either of them smile, and I never saw them smile in the same room. I was taken aback but felt a glimmer of hope, and I thought perhaps things would improve between my parents, and in particular, my relationship with them.

The scenario was awkward as I was introduced to my sister and brothers for the first time as the little sister they may or may not have known existed. I was made to shake hands as each was introduced to me. Their faces were expressionless. It seemed as if their bodies were motionless as they sat around the table in the restaurant. It was a stiff first encounter, and our relationship did not improve from there. They were no longer children; they were young adults. Sucainna was twenty-four, Raymond was twenty, and Billy was sixteen.

There was an obvious large gap in our ages, but more importantly, our life experiences were dramatically different. Although not scarred physically, they suffered deep emotional and psychological wounds. The atrocities and horrors of war traumatized my brothers and sister. They had seen dead bodies everywhere—both young and old—babies abandoned, and what I could only call the worst in humanity. They had experienced starvation, they had seen people killed in front of them, and they had survived bombings.

One time there were three boats being loaded with people attempting to flee the Japanese. My siblings, with only the clothes they wore, were in one of the overloaded vessels, crammed tightly together with other terror-filled men, women, and children. This was done late at night to avoid being seen. The boats floated out to sea in the midst of muffled screams and cries. My siblings witnessed the other two boats, one after the other, bombed in the dark in the middle of nowhere. There were no survivors. Terrified, bracing themselves for what seemed like the inevitable, they were miraculously spared.

Because my father's "gold mine" had flourished, they could finally feel safe. There was plenty of food, clothing, and money, and the dangers they once faced were now behind them. My father was overjoyed that his children were alive and back home. He gave them whatever they asked for: new clothes, fountain pens (a luxury), bicycles, schooling, and spending money. We spent most of our time downstairs in the restaurant celebrating with lots of food and visitors coming to rejoice with us over the next few weeks. Life was good.

As soon as the festivities died down, I began to see them for what they were: angry, bitter, and defensive.

The problem was that my siblings could not enjoy their new surroundings; the war still haunted them. They had been separated from their parents at a young age, and my sister Irene's death had a traumatic impact on their lives. They were resentful at life, and soon it became apparent that they were resentful toward me.

After my siblings returned home, my mother remained sober for quite a while. I was no longer her target. Unfortunately my siblings, especially my sister, became her target. Things turned real ugly fast.

They saw me as a spoiled child (perhaps I was) in comparison to what they had experienced. Raymond and Billy resented that while they were suffering in China, I was living a privileged life and lacked nothing. Because of our difference in ages and in experiences, we did not speak the same language. I, a little stranger in their midst, did not fit in.

Also, my sister and her two younger brothers bickered, quarreled, and fought with each other. I did not fully understand what they argued about, but I did know that their arguments were always centered around their years in China. Only a few months after our initial meeting, my brothers decided they wanted nothing to do with me and stopped talking to me. The chasm between us lasted throughout my childhood and into my adult years. Sadly, whatever problem we had was never resolved.

My brothers complained about me to my father and uncle. Uncle Fred and, surprisingly, my father defended me against their accusations, telling them that I was a good girl and their accusations were unfounded. My father's approval meant so much to me even though no words were exchanged between us. That did not go well with my brothers. They became angrier with me and for a while were determined to undermine me.

Maybe it was the joy of the Lord that was still with me that irritated my brothers, because they saw me as irresponsible, disrespectful, and too carefree. Yes, it bothered them that I was a happy child. My sister, Sucainna, continued to talk to me, but she only tolerated me. Her disapproving looks and angry glares frightened and hurt me. Desperate for love and acceptance, I did everything the way I thought would meet with her approval. During my teens years, I cried and cried as I gave up trying; it was impossible to break through to her heart.

Looking back, it is tragic that three people so wounded and emotionally broken lived out their lives in anger and bitterness. They—as well as my mother—never reached their potential. They lived with disillusionment and unfulfilled dreams. Oddly, in spite of their individual pain, my sister and brothers were still there for each other, even as much as they fought. At least they talked to one another.

Less than six months into their return home, my mother accused my sister of not respecting or honoring her. Her anger was like a raging inferno. She was uncontrollable as she spewed out words that brought a definitive and permanent division to the family. I came home from school that day and walked into the midst of her heated rampage. My mother directed her anger toward my sister and two brothers in the middle of the restaurant, to the horror of everyone there. Even though the language was Chinese, no interpretation was needed for the waitresses and customers. My mother was oblivious to the fact that the restaurant was a place of business and not a place for private or personal affairs. This public display of raw emotion caused my father, my sister, and my brothers and I to be stunned, motionless and speechless from the sheer magnitude of her anger. We all lost face that day.

Days after this episode, my sister was getting ready to leave the family. She had made arrangements to meet up with a man she knew, with plans on getting married. As she was going out the door with her suitcase in her hand, my mother—once again—made a huge commotion.

"We spent so much money on you to bring you here, and now you are leaving?" she yelled.

My sister hesitated at the doorway of the restaurant as my mother continued on. Sucainna put down her suitcase and struggled with what to do. Should she go against the cultural filial piety (complete obedience to our parents), or should she adhere to it? I ran to my sister, trying to help her.

"Just go, Sucainna. Don't let Mother stop you," I pleaded.

My mother had just shamed her in front of everyone at the restaurant a few days before, and now she was doing it again. I wanted my sister to be happy and away from my mother. I yelled "Go! Go! Go! Get out of here!" as I pushed her in an effort to get her to leave. My heart went out to her as she stood at the doorway, still wrestling with her emotions while my mother's wild outbursts continued. Sucainna chose to adhere to the tradition of filial piety and did not leave. Regretfully, my sister never married.

So much happened shortly after my siblings' arrival home. It set our family on a course that turned out to be irreversible. My father could not believe what was happening after the initial period of celebration and reconciliation. I'm sure he thought that with his family intact, and everyone working in the restaurant, that life would be happier. His gold mine flourished as his dreams of family life in Canada disintegrated.

I felt his sadness.

CHAPTER FIVE

THEY LOVE ME,
THEY LOVE ME NOT

My sister took me to Midnight Mass on Christmas Eve when I was nine years old. It was held in the chapel of the Chinese Missionary Catholic Church in Montreal's Chinatown. I was deeply impacted when I walked into the chapel for the first time around midnight. I was in awe as the love of God and the presence of God filled the chapel. My first impression was, Wow, God is here. I felt like I could reach out and touch God. Up until then, I did not know much about Jesus—having only vaguely heard about Jesus, and knowing even less about the cross or the Holy Spirit. I was still keenly aware of the presence of God in my life and in my surroundings. That night, His beautiful presence was like a thick mist throughout the chapel. I decided then that I wanted to become a Catholic. (It became a reality when I turned sixteen.)

The priests and nuns of that church were former missionaries in China. They spoke Chinese and also understood our culture. This was important to me. Because they understood me and the culture I grew up in, I did not have to explain myself. I wanted to be like them— loving, kind, compassionate, and patient. The chapel was a place of comfort, and I attended Sunday mass there periodically. Occasionally, I would drop in to visit during the week, always feeling welcomed and loved, which was desperately needed in my life. I am sure the priests and nuns must have prayed often for me also.

I was grateful my sister took me to church that Christmas, because later her resentment toward her family took over her life.

The following year, my parents were approached by the parents of a three-month-old boy, Tommy, asking if we would adopt him because they believed they could not afford to provide for him. They thought our family would be perfect for Tommy since we appeared wealthy and normal. His birth parents had no idea how dysfunctional my family was. My mother asked me if we should adopt the boy. I said yes only because he was so cute, and maybe I could have a good relationship with someone in the house. We adopted Tommy. My sister was given the task of caring for him, much to her displeasure. She always regretted the decision of not leaving the house that day when she could have gotten married. Now, caring for a baby she did not want, she truly became an angry and bitter person.

She fit right in with the rest of family.

DAD'S FULFILLED DREAM

My father had saved enough money to fulfill his dream to purchase his own property. He bought a three-story building in a more upscale part of the city. The new property had a restaurant within it and another store beside it, which provided a rental income. I was twelve when we moved from Atwater Street to this new location, which was a far cry from the previous place. The building was newer and well maintained. I was so grateful that there were no cockroaches or mice or rats, and it was not as dark and spooky as the two previous places I had lived in. As before, we lived on the second floor, with the restaurant beneath us and the third floor was rented out to tenants. The restaurant was given to my brothers and sister to manage. After many years of working every single day, my father was retiring and wanted to start enjoying life.

He tried to reach out to my mother in hopes of having a wife to share his leisure years with, but she was unreachable. In his efforts to please her and make her happy, he bought her many gifts and tried to do whatever she wanted. He even offered to take her to the movies, which was unheard of for him. After trying over and over to connect with his wife, though he never spoke to me, I could tell by looking at him that he realized the door to her heart was permanently closed. He had cut me out of his life for years, and now at age sixty-five, there was no one to enjoy his later years with.

TUBERCULOSIS (TB)

Shortly after my thirteenth birthday, I started my menstrual cycle. I was losing an excessive amount of blood and did not know that this was not the norm. On top of that, I was having inexplicable severe nosebleeds. I grew weaker and weaker but didn't realize the abnormal loss of blood was the cause. Since help was never readily available to me, I did not know how to reach out.

What started off with a cold progressed slowly into tuberculosis (TB) over the course of almost three years. I steadily lost weight. Standing at four foot ten, I went down from ninety pounds to seventy pounds. Much to my surprise, my mother and father were concerned about my declining health. My parents and my uncle did not believe in traditional doctors but believed in the old Chinese remedies. My father and my uncle made many bitter broths out of Chinese herbs and roots for me to drink. When my health continued to decline, my mother took me to see various doctors, but I was misdiagnosed.

Initially, the doctors thought I had a cold or the flu because of my constant cough. One doctor in particular advised healthier foods, vitamins, and a bit of wine to rebuild my strength. Another physician totally missed it. He said I was pregnant. My parents wondered about that because I had not been out of the house in almost two years except to visit the doctors. In my naivety I believed the doctor because at that age, I did not know how babies were conceived. My only logical explanation was some man deliberately caused my pregnancy while on the bus since we always traveled by bus for my doctor appointments. So convinced I was pregnant, I prayed to God and begged that He would somehow reverse the pregnancy. I cried and cried and pleaded and pleaded with God for weeks until I realized the diagnosis was wrong. What a relief that was! Later on, lumps developed around my neck. The doctors then thought it was cancer and sent me home to die. One physician sent me to have radiation treatments! After a few treatments, I discontinued them because of an inner strength within me assuring me that I did not have cancer and that I was not going to die. (I now know it was the Holy Spirit.)

However, my health continued to decline to the point of being bedridden. I no longer had any energy to climb out of bed. I could not eat—swallowing was too painful. Then one day, the Lord spoke audibly to me while I was lying in bed. He told me to go to a specific doctor who was located in an office that was part of the Catholic church in Chinatown. The Lord gave me strength to get out of bed that day. In the hot month of July, wearing a winter coat with winter clothes underneath, I took the bus there.

Upon my arrival, a nun greeted me. I said, "Sister, I am very sick. I need help."

She said I was fortunate that the doctor happened to be in that day as she led me to the next room. It must have been obvious to him that I was sick, because he did not ask me any questions or examine me. He immediately sent me to get a chest X-ray, which showed my lungs were infected with tuberculosis. He booked me into a tuberculosis hospital, which at that time was known as a sanitarium, and it was for females only. This all took place a few days short of my sixteenth birthday. I had been physically ill for almost three years before receiving a proper diagnosis.

THEY ACTUALLY DID LOVE ME

My mother accompanied me to the hospital, and as we approached the hospital ward she shared something that took me by surprise. She said, "Your father loves you." I must have given her a look of incredulity, because she continued, "He cried when you were packing your clothes to come here. He believes you are going to die here and will not come home alive."

I was taken aback. I had a hard time believing that my dad actually cried tears for me.

"But dad never shows that he loves me. He never talks to me. He always ignores me. How can he love me?"

That's when I discovered the root of the problem my father had with me. She shared that he was upset with me because he thought I did not love him enough to kiss him or hug him, referring back to the incident with the customer in the restaurant. I shamed him in front of that customer, and it caused him to lose face, and evidently that was my unforgivable crime. I was stunned. I did not know how to respond.

His uncompromising pride deprived me of a father, and my father of a loving daughter.

It was difficult to process that my father loved me. This revelation made me aware of the ten lost years living in the same house—sitting in the same room, eating at the same table, yet never a word exchanged between us. Had my mother's relationship with my father and with me been a healthy one, this situation would have been resolved. The lines of communication between us would have been opened, and I could have explained my dilemma of not knowing how to kiss or hug.

My mother also feared the worst—that I would not survive. She promised to stop drinking if my life would be spared. It was unclear to me to whom she made this promise. Did she believe in God? Did she promise Him, or did she make this promise to the Chinese gods she believed in? Amazingly, she kept her promise and never drank alcohol again. She wept profusely at the hospital. For the first time she spoke of how much I meant to her and that out of all her children, I was the only one who was never unkind to her. I did not know if my siblings were ever unkind to her, or if this was her perception.

Did she not realize the damage she herself caused in the family relationships? How could she not know?

Even though there was talk of my death, dying never entered my mind the whole time I was sick. I always knew I would recover. My inner strength was unshakable. God's Spirit sustained me and strengthened me. The revelation that death could not touch me fueled my confidence, and it was with this foreknowledge that I assured my mother that I was not going to die.

Then a feeling of anger overcame me as I became conscious that for the first time she was behaving like a loving mother would toward her daughter. I felt that it was too late for that now. I no longer wanted a mother-daughter relationship with her. So when she started whining about her other children not treating her right, I felt anger instead of sympathy. She never sowed any love or compassion into me, and I had no love or compassion to give back to her. In fact, I felt better once she left me at the hospital.

EIGHTEEN MONTHS OF PEACE

Now, most people dread staying at the hospital, but I loved being there. The peaceful atmosphere relaxed me. In comparison to the cold silence of my house, the hospital enveloped me in a loving embrace free of tension, anger, resentment, conflicts, and the swirling chaos that continually invaded our home. The nurses who looked after the patients were all nuns. At the time of my arrival, I had severe pain in my chest and throat, creating great difficulty swallowing food or water. Even swallowing my own saliva took extreme effort. When my first meal arrived, at around five in the evening, I told the nun, "I can't eat because it is too painful to swallow."

She looked at me with compassion. "Do your best, dear. Try and eat as much as you can."

I was unaccustomed to being spoken to so nicely. As I put the first bit of food into my mouth, much to my surprise, it didn't hurt to swallow. I could eat. I became aware my body felt normal and pain free. My strength returned. This all happened shortly after my arrival there. So much transpired in just a few hours—my first-time conversation with my mother, learning that my father loved me, the culture shock of moving from a home of chaos to a temporary home of peace, and now the miraculous healing of my body. I could not process it all.

The next morning I was scheduled for another chest X-ray. Again, I heard the audible voice of God. He said to me, "I have healed you, but the X-rays will show that you are still sick."

I was mystified. Why did God heal me and yet it would appear that I still had tuberculosis?

It did not make sense. In hindsight, I wonder if this was God's way of granting me a respite from the madness that was going on at home.

DEMONIC PRESENCE

Being the youngest patient, I received extra attention from the nuns. The room I was assigned to had three empty beds. I was given the choice of beds and chose the one by the window. One of the nuns was concerned that I would be afraid to sleep alone, so she prepared me for what to expect in the evenings.

"Bedtime is at eight o'clock. The lights will go off, and shortly thereafter the night watchman will walk by with a lantern. He will walk throughout the halls and then make his way back. He will exit through the doorway that he first came through, and you will hear the door slam, but this is the only noise you will hear all night."

She assured me that she would keep my bedroom door opened and that she would be in the office near my room. She promised me that she would be there if I should need anything. What a new experience— someone concerned about me!

Eight o'clock came and the lights were turned off. I laid down to sleep, and like clockwork I heard the night watchman start his walk. I saw the light from his lantern and heard his footsteps as he made his rounds throughout the hospital. Then I heard him leave through the same door he had come in. Everything happened exactly as the nun said.

Immediately after the night watchman made his exit, a presence came down on me. My first instinct was that it was the night watchman. Then I thought, It can't be the night watchman. I heard him in the hallway. I heard his distant steps as he made his way to the door. I heard the distant sound of the door opening and closing. Within seconds, I felt arms clenched around me. Trying to understand what this "thing" was, I reasoned to myself that if it were a human being, I would have to be lifted off the bed in order to have arms wrapped around me. Also, I didn't feel my bed being flattened by any weight; the weight was entirely on my body. Knowing the nun was close by in her office, I tried to cry out to her, but no sound came out of my mouth. I tried to wiggle out from under the malevolent weight but felt paralyzed. I tried moving my arms, legs, torso, and my head but could not move any part of my body. Perhaps I was dreaming, but I was able to move my eyes and see every detail of the bed sheets, the blanket, the color of the wall, and the light that came in through the window. There wasn't any doubt in my mind that I was awake and this strange thing was real. Somehow, I knew I could communicate mentally with this thing that was gripping me.

"What do you want?" I asked it.

Immediately, it started pulling me through the bed— not off the bed, but through the bed. I could not make a sound or a movement. Its grip tightened, and that was when I became acutely aware of the danger. Wherever it wanted to take me, I knew I didn't want to go there. I had no idea what that thing or spirit was, nor did I care. All I wanted was for it to leave—immediately. The only prayer I knew was the "Our Father," which I learned at school, and since no sound came from my vocal chords, I mentally said the prayer slowly.

"Our Father, who art in heaven..." I paused and waited. Nothing happened.

"Hallowed be Thy name. Thy kingdom come..."

I paused and waited. Nothing changed. "Thy will be done, on earth as it is in heaven."

Nothing.

Fear was starting to get the best of me. "Give us this day, our daily bread..."

Nothing.

It wasn't until I mentally said "Deliver us from evil..." that the spirit left—as quickly as it had come.

Immediately, I felt comforted by the Holy Spirit and fell asleep peacefully.

Not long after my initial arrival, two other ladies joined me in my room. We quickly became friends, not only with each other, but with other patients as well. Most of us were long-term residents, ranging anywhere from two months to a few years. Oftentimes, we would hear shouts of joy and cries of celebration when the doctor, during his weekly visit, would discharge a person with a clean bill of health.

My stay at the hospital lasted a year and a half. My mother and father never visited me.

I did not expect them to.

The other patients all had visitors come and go. Some brought flowers. Some brought food and great-looking desserts, but mostly they brought much-needed conversation.

I watched the interactions between the patients and their family and friends, their smiles, their affections, and their warmth toward each other. I really longed for that.

I quickly learned what normal family life could be and should be like as I interacted with the other patients. The open communications, hearing their stories of their lives at home, and just being able to laugh and be supportive of each other. I was learning about life outside of the only life I knew.

Unlike the other ladies, I had no family stories to share and no heartwarming memories to reminisce about. It embarrassed me that I could not exchange childhood stories or fond memories with them. My family was nothing to be proud about, and I felt so ashamedly different from this new community.

The hospital itself was not a large place. There were about thirty-five rooms, each with two to four beds per room. We shared three communal bathroom facilities. It was not a place where I could isolate myself...not that I wanted to. Another reason why I loved my stay there.

The following year was my conversion to Catholicism. My First Communion took place in the chapel next to the hospital—a special and beautiful moment for me. All the patients, in their pajamas and housecoats, attended and were like a family to me. The sound of angelic voices singing filled the chapel. I was unbelievably happy, and my love of God overflowed.

MY BIG CHANCE

At Christmastime, the patients were allowed to go home to their families for a few days. Since the day I found out that my father loved me, this big moment was formulated in my mind because I was determined to let my dad know that I loved him. I bought my dad a tie, wrapped it in Christmas wrapping paper, and wrote him a Christmas card. With fierce determination to clarify the misunderstanding that occurred between us that fateful day, I mentally rehearsed over a hundred times what I would say to him. As the day came closer, overwhelming fear gripped me, and I knew it prevented me from telling my side of the story. Nervous, my courage quickly slipped away. I threw out the original plan and came up with another one. I would just give him the tie and the card and a big hug and a kiss, and hopefully have enough courage to tell him I loved him. My goal was to tell my father I had always loved him.

It seemed simple enough.

On the way home, my nervousness and fears drove me to come up with another plan, which again, I mentally practiced. Upon seeing him, I would smile and say, "Merry Christmas, Baba. I love you." Then I would give him the tie and the card but not the hug and not the kiss.

Hopefully there would be some reaction from my dad.

Upon entering our apartment, I saw him sitting in the room that was a combination of kitchen, eating area, sitting area, and laundry room. He stoically read the newspaper. My heart stopped for a moment and so did my feet. Fear paralyzed me, and I was at a loss on what to do. Standing at the entryway, he must have known I was there, but he didn't even look up from his paper. With consummate effort, I forced myself to enter the room, but when he didn't acknowledge me, I walked right out. I stood there for a moment and fought my fear and managed to walk back into the room and began to pace back and forth. He continued to read the newspaper. I courageously walked around him, trying to get his attention, but got nothing. My feet purposely made noise as I circled him again. Positioning myself behind him, I figured I would just hug him from behind so that I would not see his face.

I just wanted my dad to know that I loved him so much.

Those moments were an eternity for me. I was having a difficult time overcoming the fear of being spurned, ignored, and rejected again. The trauma of my father's rejection at a young age had a more debilitating effect on me than I realized.

As I was battling myself in my mind, he startled me. "What's wrong with you. Why are you pacing the floor?" he said in Chinese, clearly annoyed.

He hadn't seen me in so long. I was only there for a few days because it was Christmastime, and that was the first thing he said to me? Overwhelmed with fear, I couldn't respond. His look of annoyance destroyed any hope I had of an emotional reconciliation. I ended up walking out of the room, defeated. I never gave him the tie or the card that took me forever to write. I never told him how much I loved him.

This was my one big chance, and I blew it. Another thick layer of pain settled over my buried heart. After a few days home, I was happy to go back to the hospital.

BACK TO ISOLATION

Eighteen months had gone by before my mother came to see me. She cried and pleaded for me to come back home. She needed me. My sister and brothers were now running the family business, and she was not allowed to go downstairs to the restaurant. I thought, What did she do now? She must have done something seriously wrong to be confined to her apartment, almost like a forced imprisonment. I discharged myself against the wishes of the doctors and the nuns—maybe I did have some compassion for her after all.

However, it was a decision I regretted many times over. How I longed to go back to the hospital, but I couldn't.

The family dynamics had shifted during my absence. It was as if in one corner were my father and brothers; my mother and I were in another. My father and my brothers wanted nothing to do with us. My sister was always civil to my mother and me.

The role of being my mother's caretaker somehow fell on my shoulders. It was hard for me to fulfill her needs, since my own needs were never met. Still, she became extremely dependent on me and relied on me for everything. She actually talked to me like a normal person at times. I was not emotionally invested in our relationship and just did my duty.

My mother and I hibernated upstairs in our living quarters, and I only went downstairs to the restaurant for food for both of us. My father and brothers made us feel like intruders in the family's restaurant.

DEMONIC ENCOUNTERS

If it wasn't bad enough that I grew up in such a dysfunctional family, to add to the craziness of my home life, demonic figures haunted me as far back as I can remember. The demon who tried to grab me at the hospital was not my first such confrontation.

When I was about eight years old, I had a mysterious experience similar to the one Raymond had as a young boy. Whether it would have been life threatening or not forever remains a mystery. When the restaurant had coal delivered, the coal was poured into a chute linked to a room next to the kitchen. One day when I was walking past this room, the door was ajar. I was about eight to ten feet away from it. The mountain of coal could be seen through the opening of the door. On top of the pile of coal was a figure that looked like a fairy or an imp. It was completely black, like the mountain of coal on which it was sitting. The room was as dark as night, yet I was able to see clearly into it. This figure surprised me when it beckoned me with its finger, mesmerizing me. I did not want to go inside the room but could not control my body or my feet. I was aware that my feet were making their way toward the room but was powerless to stop them, as if they were not my own. Uncle Fred walked by and saw me. He slammed the door shut and locked it saying, "Don't go in there. It's dirty. You'll get your dress dirty." As the door slammed, the hypnotic trance was broken, and I was jolted back to reality.

Living in the apartment above the restaurant across from the Atwater Market was a daily challenge. Thirty or forty demons (I counted them!) chased me every time I made my way upstairs to our living quarters. I could never walk up the stairs—I always ran as fast as I could to get away from them. Coming down the flight of stairs, they lunged at me. They hounded me and terrorized me day and night. I suffered terrible nightmares. I would awaken in a cold sweat in the middle of the night to see demonic spirits staring right in my face. Not only were they visible to me, but I was able to feel the hatred and horrible emotions those spirits emitted. At times they would grab me. Thinking it was a human being, I would jump and shake myself loose only to find that no one else was around.

I did not have the proper vocabulary or the understanding to express to anyone this phenomenon until many years later when I learned about the spiritual realm of angelic and demonic beings. The spirits that tormented me came in all shapes and sizes. Some were tall, some were short, some looked like fairies. Others were ugly trolls or imps. They followed me everywhere—it didn't matter if I was at a store or if we moved to another house or when moving to another city. I was harassed without any respite.

Growing into adulthood, the demonic experiences intensified. I experienced being raped while sleeping at night—my body paralyzed and powerless to stop it.

I always ignored it, thinking they were bad dreams and an ultra-vivid imagination, until the 1990s, when the Lord revealed to me that these experiences were real. This revelation shocked me beyond words. I began to battle them through prayer and counseling, and though the rape stopped, the demonic harassment continued. I pleaded and prayed for God to intervene. It had been going on for decades, to the point where I started to think that this was just something I was going to have to endure for the rest of my life. Perhaps this was to be my "thorn in the flesh" that the apostle Paul wrote about in 2 Corinthians 12:7–10:

> And lest I should be exalted above measure by the abundance of the revelations, a thorn in the flesh was given to me, a messenger of Satan to buffet me, lest I be exalted above measure.
>
> Concerning this thing I pleaded with the Lord three times that it might depart from me.
>
> And He said to me, "My grace is sufficient for you, for My strength is made perfect in weakness." Therefore most gladly I will rather boast in my infirmities, that the power of Christ may rest upon me.

Therefore I take pleasure in infirmities, in reproaches, in needs, in persecutions, in distresses, for Christ's sake. For when I am weak, then I am strong.

There was a time when my sanity was being challenged, I feared for my life. The demonic spirits seemed to be coming at me with such force, they actually threatened me with death. One day, around the year 2000, the sovereign hand of God showed up in a powerful way. God completely removed them from my life, and I was free. The battle truly belongs to the Lord.

CHAPTER SIX

MORE DISAPPOINTMENTS

t eighteen, in an attempt to break free of my family, I ventured out on my own and found a job in a large department store for the Christmas season. I worked in the shipping department, packaging parcels that were to be delivered to customers' homes. Sometimes I helped the cashiers wrap the purchases for the customers. After the holiday season ended, the manager asked if I would consider staying on full time. She wanted to train me to be a cashier because she was pleased with my work ethic and my attitude. I didn't mind working in the shipping department or helping the cashiers, because very little interaction with people was required.

By now, my fears overwhelmed me. I was petrified even thinking of dealing with the public. I thanked her for the offer but did not take it. I just couldn't do it.

A few months later, I responded to an ad in the paper for a job in an insurance company, and I was quickly hired. I may have made about nine dollars a week. I worked in the mailroom, sorting and delivering letters or parcels to the different departments. I ran errands and did little odd jobs around the office. I enjoyed working in an office environment, although it was unfamiliar to me since I had never stepped into an office building before. Though afraid, it was not as frightening as interacting with the public in a department store. Whatever I did not understand was always patiently explained to me. No one was ever upset when I made mistakes. I had trouble telling apart an invoice from a statement, but the ladies didn't appear to mind explaining it to me on more than a few occasions.

I had found a job that psychologically I could handle, but for some reason my father did not approve. To this day, I still do not know his reason. Whatever my father had to say to me was always communicated to my mother, and she would relay the message to me. That was how I communicated back with my father. When I insisted on keeping the job, he then wanted me to pay him rent and to buy my own food. I would no longer be allowed to eat at home. We both knew that I did not make enough money to fulfill his demands. On top of that, I knew my father would make it really hard for me if I went against his will. It was with great reluctance that I gave my notice to my employers. They surprised me by asking me to reconsider. They wanted to know if I was leaving because I was unhappy working there. If so, what could they do to improve my situation?

One supervisor—the sincerity in his voice so touched me—expressed his belief in my capabilities and how I was a great fit with the company. He shared with me how the president of the firm started at the bottom and climbed the corporate ladder, and how he rose to become the president. Everyone there saw potential in me and was willing to teach and help me.

I did not know how to process these encouraging words, words that told me that I was smart and

I had potential. That people would treat me like I was important was surprising to me.

I did not know how to respond to their sincerity and kindness.

I knew I was losing out on a great opportunity, and I wanted to let them know that it wasn't their fault, but how could I explain my situation at home when I didn't fully understand it? With great regret, I thanked them for everything, and without telling them the real reason, I left them and the job to return to my emotional bondage. To this day, I still remember the wonderful people there. Many times I would go on to think about how different my life would have been had I been allowed to take the opportunity. Once again, I was devastated.

I did nothing for many months after that. I was not even allowed to go downstairs to the restaurant to help out. A mantle of misery cloaked me. There was just my mother and I with no other external contact or communication. We did not have a television to help pass the time away. I was bored and saw no hope or a way out of my situation. Then a relative of ours asked my father if I could work as a cashier for a Chinese restaurant in which he was part owner. Begrudgingly, my father consented, and I worked there for a few years. My contact with people was minimal since being a cashier at that restaurant only involved making change for people as they paid their bills. My father left me alone as I worked for this relative and did not require any money from me.

Working at the restaurant helped fill in time, for which I was so grateful.

DAD GIVES UP

My father made every effort to get my mother and my siblings to reconcile their differences. It was an impossible task since there was no forgiveness or love or acceptance on either side. He decided to leave his family and move to Hong Kong in an effort to find peace in his remaining years.

He bought a two-story building that housed four apartments in Hong Kong. I found out after the fact that he wanted my little brother, Tommy, and I to go and live with him. Tommy quickly refused to leave our sister. Unknown to me, my sister and my mother made the decision that I was to stay with my mother. I was upset when I found out that there was a conversation going on about me and my life and I was not part of the conversation and not part of the decisions made on my behalf. I was so shattered when my father left without me, because any chance of restoring my relationship with my father left with him.

It would have been the ideal opportunity for us to get to know each other all over again and perhaps rekindle the relationship we once had.

However...my sister told me I had to stay with my mother because there was no one else who would take care of her. Because of the open hostility and hatred between her and her other children, I was still the only one who would bother to tend to her. Besides, my mother would not have let me go. In her own way, I think she really loved me.

I am grateful to God for the circumstances that prevented me from going to Hong Kong with my father. Years later, my father was murdered. My life could have been in jeopardy had I been there. The perpetrators took over the house and whatever money he had. We were told not to try to seek justice because of the danger involved. Sadly, my father died never knowing the truth about my deep love for him.

ENOUGH IS ENOUGH

Like my dad, I finally reached a point where I had enough of the family. The joy of the Lord somehow got buried amid the pain and was forgotten.

At twenty-two years old, I took the bold step to leave home and to leave my mother.

She was so dependent on me that it seemed like her full weight was upon me.

Physically and emotionally worn out, I could no longer care for her. She would have to fend for herself. In leaving home, I left behind my past and hoped to create a better life for myself. Confused, unhappy, and lost, I left at the spur of the moment without any concrete plans. In hindsight, God orchestrated my path.

I bought a one-way ticket to Toronto since it was not too far away, only about 320 miles. I had not developed the ability to exercise sound judgment or common sense.

Had God not been protecting me, my journey into the unknown could have been disastrous. The bus reached its destination in the downtown area at ten o'clock at night. With my suitcase in tow, a true stranger to a big city, I searched for a place to stay. Downtown Toronto was not the safest place for a young girl to walk around in, especially late at night, but I was unaware of the potential danger. Seeing a house that had a room to rent, I went in and rented the room for the night. I gave the landlord all the money I had for one night's rent, leaving me with ten cents left. Perhaps it was the Holy Spirit, or perhaps it was my ignorance, but having only ten cents left and not knowing how I was going to survive, I was not afraid or concerned. After settling my things into the room, I walked towards the main street and saw a sign in the window of a restaurant that said Waitress Wanted. I applied, got the job, and was to start work the next day. With the money I made in tips, there was just enough for my next day's rent. The restaurant provided a free meal each day I worked. With my first pay check, I rented a room at a women's dormitory close by. I was able to pay for a week's rent and relied on my tips to see me through the week.

My life till then had been sheltered, so I was naive and innocent. Angels must have worked overtime to protect me. I thought everyone was trustworthy and honest. Once, while walking to work, a man started talking to me and invited me to his place for a barbecue that weekend. I agreed to go, thinking what a kind and friendly person he was. It never crossed my mind that his motives may not be as pure as I perceived them to be. When I told some of the other waitresses at the restaurant of my encounter with this stranger, they adamantly warned me against going to his place. They advised me against being too trusting and not to go out with strangers.

Being new to Toronto, I liked to go for walks to familiarize myself with the city. One evening I walked around an area not knowing it was the "red light district." I did not know such an area even existed, but unbeknownst to me, God was looking after me. A customer, who recognized me from the restaurant where I worked, saw me there and warned me of the dangers of the area and the implications of my being there. I quickly left and headed to my room. I did not venture out too often after that except to walk to and from work, which was only a block away.

Being on my own for the first time brought new challenges, especially financial ones.

I agreed to work my regular evening hours plus the lunch hours so I could earn more money and could eat the meals allowed by the restaurant.

The hostess was a lady with a mother's heart. She may have seen how immature and gullible I was. She seemed to watch over me, especially since most of the clientele were men. The restaurant was in the heart of the downtown area surrounded by nightclubs, topless clubs, and other unsavory places. She advised me not to believe everything the men said and to beware of their motives.

Another challenge was trying to be normal, to fit in. I felt so lost—I did not really know how to function in work relationships. It was like being a little girl trying to live in an adult world.

Unaware that there was anything wrong with me, I believed this was life and I needed to learn how to live it the best I could.

Desperation overruled my many fears. I was determined to succeed in establishing a happy life for myself. There was no way I was ever going back to my family. I had no choice but to plow through.

MARRIAGE: HISTORY REPEATS ITSELF

On a day off I went to a Chinese restaurant that was close by for a bite to eat. There, I met Wilbert Lowe, who was part owner. He struck a conversation with me and before I knew it, he asked me out. Though I had been previously warned about going out with strangers, I agreed to go out with Wilbert because he was Chinese, and I felt safe with my own people. We dated for only two weeks when he asked me to marry him.

He was twenty-seven years older than me and a widower with five children. In a sweet voice I told him, "Wilbert, I am not ready to get married." I had zero intentions of following in my mother's footsteps.

Somehow he misunderstood what I said and took my answer as a yes and got excited. I looked at him in disbelief as he started rambling on joyfully about our future together, and I did not have the heart to tell him that my response was actually no to his marriage proposal. In hindsight, I do not know what would have happened to me if I had not married him, because the reality was, I could not take care of myself emotionally or financially. I was ill equipped to survive on my own in a strange city for too long.

History was repeating itself and I had no idea if it was God's will. In spite of my best intentions, I walked right in my mother's footsteps.

About a month later, Wilbert and I were married. I fervently prayed to God that He would help me through life as a married woman and as a mother to three boys and two girls—Victor, Vincent, and Vernon, and Virginia and Rosanne—whose ages ranged from six to seventeen.

I was absolutely clueless in my new role as wife and mother. I went from living in a form of isolation to a packed house. I never had any reason to cook, nor were there any opportunities to learn. My meals were always ready made from the family restaurant. Wilbert had to teach me how to cook. I never saw my mother clean, dust, or tidy the house, so Wilbert taught me how to clean the house. He patiently taught me all the things I should have known how to do.

However, I also did not know how to be a mother, and he couldn't teach me that.

Wilbert was a popular man in the Chinese community, and he received many invitations to weddings or other social functions. With much dread, I accompanied him and tried to socialize. I explained to him that the only social function I had ever attended was when I was about six years old. I did not know how to make small talk or engage in conversation. Plus, I felt awkward in Chinese functions. I did not know the Chinese protocols and social formalities. My command of the Chinese language was insufficient since conversation with my parents and siblings was almost nonexistent. He understood all of that and agreed to speak for me. When anyone approached me and tried to start a conversation, he spoke on my behalf. Whenever he used the restroom, I hid in the ladies' room and waited for him to come out. I was terrified that someone might try to engage in conversation with me. Not only was Wilbert understanding of my situation, he never shamed or teased me about my shortcomings.

A few years later, for the first time, I realized something was wrong with me. A lady had collapsed on the sidewalk, and there was a crowd of people trying to help. I looked at the faces of the people surrounding her. It appeared that they genuinely cared about this woman; concern and compassion were in their expressions. I was shocked to discover my lack of emotions.

I didn't care for this lady who obviously needed help.

My heart was as hard as the sidewalk the lady had collapsed on. I came to the conclusion that God must have made a mistake when He created me, that He forgot to give me emotions. I became aware that I didn't have love, hate, empathy, or any other feeling for myself or for anyone else.

It was a horrible revelation, and although I did not want to live that way, that was the way I was. And nothing could be done about it.

Not too long afterward, depression sank over me, and I didn't understand why. I could not stop crying, and staying awake became problematic. My doctor prescribed medications, but I didn't take them for long because they made me feel numb and lethargic. I was no longer able to help at the restaurant that Wilbert had bought. Thoughts of suicide invaded my mind, but the fear of going to hell prevented me from killing myself. So I prayed to God that He would take my life and somehow He would allow me to die in my sleep. Each morning I faced the disappointment that God didn't answer my prayer. About a year later, as if the Holy Spirit kicked me out of my despair, I made a decision.

"Lord," I said, "since You will not let me die, then I am going to make the best of my life while I can." That ended my depression. I wasn't going to feel sorry for myself anymore.

During the early years of my marriage, I became chronically fatigued. I could barely move; my body felt heavy and exhausted. I also battled sleepiness. I could not get enough sleep. I needed at least twelve hours of sleep every night. Many weekends were literally lost in sleep. I was falling asleep during the daytime no matter how much sleep I had at night. My doctor suggested that

I begin to exercise. But exercising at the gym made me feel worse. I was sleeping my life away. I felt like I was the only one in the world who had the type of problems I had. To me, everyone else was normal—everyone but me.

(The Lord healed me instantly in 1995 from chronic fatigue. It was another ten years later when the Lord healed me of chronic sleepiness, though not instantly, but in stages.)

Seven years into our marriage, we realized that I was not able to conceive. We applied to adopt a child. After a two-year wait, Valerie, who was almost seven months old, came into our lives. I knew God chose her for us, as my happiness returned. We adopted a second child, and we brought four-month-old Lynn home. Once again, I felt God's hand in bringing her to us. Our precious little ones brought me so much joy even though, like my mother before me, I did not really know what to do with babies.

Valerie was with us for about a week, and I was wrestling with how to care for her. She was not a doll; she was a living baby with real needs. God intervened and suddenly I knew what to do. I won't say that I knew everything, but at least enough to be able to be a mother and to have some of the instincts of a mother.

I forced myself to talk and to interact with Valerie and Lynn. My biggest fear was that they would grow up to be like me. Living in silence and isolation for most of my life, I needed to remind myself to make an effort to be more involved with them. I drew a blank when it came to playing and interacting with children.

(It would be some thirty or more years later when Valerie taught me how to interact with her daughter, Megan, and later with her son, Ethan. Even with Valerie's encouragement and direction, it was not easy.)

Thankfully, my other children were supportive and helpful with their new baby sisters. They played a large and positive role in shaping their siblings' lives. I don't know what I would have done without them.

I was fiercely adamant that Valerie and Lynn would grow up to become normal adults and not in any way emulate my life. My desperate desire for them was to have the happiness and confidence that eluded me. This desire was so strong that it pushed me out of my comfort zone to interact and care for them. There were many,

many mistakes made because I functioned almost blindly without any concrete direction.

Though I did not neglect them as I was neglected, I was extremely afraid of making mistakes with Valerie and Lynn. I overcompensated for my insecurities by spoiling them and never properly teaching them or disciplining them. Wilbert helped me in so many ways and in particular when it came to childhood illnesses, such as colds, fevers, measles, and even tummy aches.

Knowing there was so much I did not understand about raising girls caused me to constantly panic. My fears, though, did drive me to pray in desperation that God would help them to become healthy and normal functioning adults.

But my childhood experiences crippled me emotionally, and I became an emotionally crippled mom who would in turn cripple her own children.

OTHER CHALLENGES

Terrified of the dark, I slept with the lights on.

I interpreted normal silence as *this person is mad at me and must hate me*. Anger, yelling, and screaming, as sometimes happens within families, terrified me. (I still cannot be in the same room with angry people.)

Panic surged through me when seeing anyone who resembled my mother—short, overweight, whiny, and highly dependent.

I couldn't perform even the simplest household task, such as dusting or arranging decorations. Housework overwhelmed me. If I scrubbed floors or vacuumed or dusted, I would go over and over and over the areas, trying for perfection. Many times, I rehearsed the process of cleaning a certain area—I would have to talk myself into it.

But in the end, I couldn't clean anything perfectly, and I gave up before trying.

(Now, the Lord did sovereignly heal me of this inability to do housework in 1999. The cupboard underneath the sink was dirty, messy, and just plain yucky. I would close my eyes to it because I could not deal with it. One day, without thinking, I knelt down and started cleaning it.

I was surprised and excited as I realized that I was doing something that was so very impossible for me. In an instant, the Lord moved this mountain of impossibility for me.)

MY SEARCH

Along with my challenges, I struggled through chronic fatigue, sleepiness, bouts of panic, anxieties, and fears, and at the same time I tried to care for my family with some kind of balance and normalcy. I heard about yoga exercises and thought to give yoga a try in the hopes it would help me defeat my battles. During one of the classes, the instructor talked about meditation. I thought, Great, I'll do the exercises, and when everybody starts meditating, I'll skip out. I was only interested in the physical aspects of yoga anyway. When the time for meditation came, the instructor turned down the lights and began speaking. A joy and a peace that I had never felt before came upon me. I was instantly hooked on yoga and especially meditation.

For the next fifteen years, I believed the lie that yoga was the answer that I had been searching for my whole life. It turned out to be a false joy and a fleeting peace as I continued to struggle with my inner turmoil and pain.

A LOSING BATTLE

Wilbert had his emotional baggage as well. Like so many couples, we were two dysfunctional people struggling with our own issues, trying to make our marriage work. I was able to see with spiritual eyes what was going on in the demonic spirit realm. I saw the demons in our marriage and in Wilbert's restaurant business. It was this reality that I was aware of and wrestled with. Without any understanding as to the reason behind it or how to deal with it, I blindly tried to fight those demons. I told them they would not win and that I would fight them with everything I had. I thought I could win by sheer willpower, by working extra-long hours, and by doing whatever needed to be done to make the restaurant run smoothly. I also tried to be extra supportive of my husband. It was as if I had boxing gloves on and was punching aimlessly in the air.

Unfortunately, they did win, and I gave up. Everything ended in disaster. The restaurant business failed no matter how hard we worked. We had plenty of customers. We had the finances. But finances were being drained away by the need to constantly maintain and upkeep the operation—overhead costs. The air conditioners gave out, the dishwashers broke, the refrigerators stopped working, and the plumbing needed constant repair.

The battle to keep the restaurant business going was futile, as was the fight to keep our marriage strong and intact.

I never doubted God's existence, because I always felt His presence through everything I experienced. Through the years, the Lord always assured me that everything would be okay. However, I did not see any evidence of God intervening in our situation. Why did the restaurant business have to fail? We had a great location with a steady clientele. With its failure came loss of face for both of us. The worst part of this was I believed there was no way out for me. I was in a trapped and hopeless pit.

At the time I had no way of knowing that the Lord was helping me in unseen ways.

I became angry and impatient as I sought a way out of my misery. I also started to feel like I was losing my grip, as if I did not have anything to hold on to—like a ship without an anchor, and the waves were taking me wherever they wanted, and I didn't have a say in it.

In 1976, after seventeen years of marriage, I left my husband and took Valerie and Lynn with me back to Montreal. They were eight and ten years old.

Once again, I ran away from my problems because I did not know how to face them.

Regretfully, this was just one of my many mistakes. The problems that I dealt with I would have faced anywhere because they were internal. I did not know that then, nor did I know the root cause of them.

I was unhappy and desperately looking for a way to fix this.

I settled in Montreal with my daughters—oblivious to the pain and damage I was doing to Valerie and Lynn by forcing them to leave their dad, their siblings, their home, their friends, and everything they knew. The long-term damage I did to them by leaving them alone to fend for themselves while I worked as a waitress in a downtown restaurant was immeasurable. Suddenly, they found themselves alone in the apartment while I worked the midnight shift. Previously surrounded by parents and siblings, they were now alone and scared. No one was there for them in case they needed help. Everything familiar had disappeared, and their routine was abruptly dismantled.

However, I was in blind pursuit of personal peace, and I did not care who or what stood in my way. I became self-absorbed, and I was prepared to sacrifice my children's happiness. But peace eluded me.

We were all taken aback and saddened when Wilbert passed away unexpectedly in 1982.

I loved Montreal. It has its own unique flavor that is not found anywhere else—*la joie de vivre*, or the joy of life. When Wilbert died, I felt an unusually strong urge to return to Toronto. Reluctantly, I left Montreal, not knowing the Holy Spirit was orchestrating my path.

Soon, I would have a real encounter with my Creator.

My father standing in
front of his nightclub

My mother

My siblings

My uncle Fred

Me and my father at Belmont park

Me standing in front of the restaurant

Me as a child

Me smiling

Me with sunglasses

Dad's dream fulfilled

Interior of the dream restaurant

My wedding

Me and Wilbert

Valerie, Wilbert, and me

Valerie, Lynn, and myself

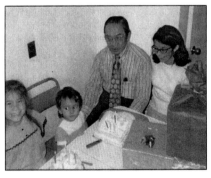

Wilbert, Valerie, Lynn, and myself

CHAPTER SEVEN

AN ENCOUNTER WITH JESUS

Ever since my dad shared with me the existence of God and the love of God, the Lord supernaturally revealed Himself to me in many ways. I had gone through much pain and heartache, through embarrassments and shame, through demonic violations and emotional turmoil, but I had always felt God's presence in and around me. The joy of the Lord had been suppressed and forgotten long ago, but His presence never left me.

Six months after my husband passed away, the Lord withdrew His presence from me. I could not live without His presence. It was the only sliver of hope and strength that I held on to throughout my entire life. Words cannot adequately describe the sense of loss. I could no longer see or feel the presence of the Lord. A complete emptiness and a sense of dryness permeated my being. It was like I was an empty shell of a person.

I became angry with God—livid, enraged. I yelled and cried to God, "This is not fair. I do not deserve this. I have been through so much. Why have You taken Your presence from me? Why can't I feel Your presence anymore?"

How was I going to live without being in the shadow of His presence? Out of everything horrible that I had experienced, this was the worst. It felt like the essence of life was drained from me. It was unbearable, and I was frantic. God's presence was more vital to me than life itself.

Struggling to cope and to meet Valerie and Lynn's needs—they were now about sixteen and fourteen years old—I held on to a cobweb thread of sanity to keep from being sucked into a black hole of depression. How long could I hang on? The void in my life was so strong that I believed the Lord had truly left me and He did not hear me. It felt like my closest friend who was always beside me was no longer there.

One evening, around ten o'clock, as I was about to drift off to sleep, I heard a male voice call my name. "Mimi." Frightened, I instinctively pulled the bed covers over my head, having no idea how a man got into my house—into my room—and how did he know my name? As I closed my eyes, hoping this was my imagination, I heard the voice again: "Mimi." I knew something was different, and because the girls were sleeping, it couldn't have been one of them. Could it be God? I slowly pulled the covers down and sat up in bed. To my amazement, Jesus was standing in front of me.

"What do You want?" I responded angrily.

"Mimi, will you serve Me?" He asked.

My life experiences shaped my own theology about God and Jesus. Since God never helped me or answered my many cries for help (or so I thought), it was because He was not concerned about me and my daily battles. He didn't intervene in the way I wanted or expected, so I figured He was busy doing things far more important than dealing with little ol' me, such as looking after nations, world affairs, wars, famine, and global crises. He must have forgotten about me, and if I was insignificant for my family, then I was surely too insignificant for the Almighty.

It was with this mind-set that I responded to Jesus' question. "Now that You are here, You are going to have to listen to what I have to say"—as if He was oblivious to the struggles I was dealing with. "I go to church. I pray. I pray to You every day. Do You ever even hear my prayers? Where have You been all these years? There are a lot of people out there who curse You. They deny Your existence, while I try to serve You. But they are living a much happier life than I have been my whole life. And on top of all I have been through, You withdrew Your presence from me. What did I do to deserve that?"

I went on to tell Jesus what a good person I was and how I totally did not deserve the life of hardship that was dealt to me. I poured out my heart because I believed that He had forgotten about my existence, and this was perhaps my only chance to tell Him what I thought of Him.

"No!" I yelled. "I will not serve You. I will never, ever, ever serve You."

Jesus left and came back the next evening at about the same time. He called my name. "Mimi." I sat up in bed, incredulous to see Him again after I had been so angry with Him.

"What do You want?" I asked again, still angry.

"Will you serve Me?" He asked.

"No. Go away and leave me alone," I answered. My anger toward Him had not subsided.

Jesus left, only to come back the next evening. He wasn't giving up, for which I am eternally grateful. Again the same scenario took place, but this time the outcome was different.

"Mimi, will you serve Me?"

My mouth opened to respond. I was going to tell Him no for the third time. However, before the word came out of my mouth, the Holy Spirit zapped me like a bolt of lightning. I was instantly filled with joy—His joy. This was a more intense joy than I had felt when I was a kid, and certainly different from the joy I had felt when I tried yoga. This powerful joy of the Lord filled me entirely.

"Do I have a choice?" I asked the Lord with an uncontainable smile pulling at my lips. Before He could respond I blurted, "Yes, yes Lord Jesus, I will serve You."

Jesus shared that I would never go back to my old way of life and what I had just experienced was a new birth. His overwhelming joy pulsated within me, and I barely could take in His words. One of His promises to me was that He would bless me. I did not understand the word "bless," but I was in awe and speechless as He continued to speak. Overpowered by His presence and His love, my anger, frustration, and depression were washed away. My mind was renewed.

I fell asleep peacefully for the first time in many years. I fell asleep with hope.

The next day, I walked outside. To my amazement, throngs of birds were on the tree branches, and they were chirping loudly in unison, happy for me. They were singing songs of joy over me. I marveled as I stood and listened to them. Then I saw a host of angels in the sky, singing. They too were rejoicing over me. I wondered, "What in the world is going on?" I looked around and saw that the leaves on the trees appeared greener than before, the sky was bluer, and even the clouds were whiter than ever. For a moment I thought I had gone insane or that it was all a dream

The peace and joy within me was undeniably real, and most importantly, His presence was back.

In my naivety I expected my circumstances to change overnight, but they didn't. My late husband did not have any insurance, and I had to borrow money to cover the funeral expenses. Working as a waitress at two jobs, it was a struggle to feed and clothe my children and to cover their school expenses as well the expenses of everyday living.

Also, relating to my daughters was challenging. It was hard enough relating to them as children, now they were teenage girls who had just lost their father, which made things even more difficult.

Because of my traumatic upbringing, I seemed to have lost my childhood and my teenage years and all the experiences that go along with them—communication, relationships, interactions, and the carefree life of being a kid and a teenager. My childhood family dynamic did not provide me with positive, solid, basic experiences to fall back on. Relating not only to Valerie and Lynn but to people in general proved problematic, because unknowingly, my emotions were suppressed. It would be about thirteen years after my encounter with Jesus that my emotions would surface and the healing process would begin to take place.

I started to wonder why Jesus wasn't helping me with this mess. I felt great inside, but other than that, nothing really changed.

I continued working two jobs, juggling my finances to make ends meet, and trying to understand two teenagers who were going through their teenage phases, which to this day, I still do not understand. Here I was in my midforties, and I did not have a firm grip on life, and my emotional state was as shaky as always.

Less than a year later, I woke up on a Saturday morning, and as usual, I started complaining to God. "God, I don't understand. I have peace in my heart because of You. I have joy because of You, but my circumstances, Lord—You don't seem to be helping me at all with the circumstances I find myself in."

I heard the Lord say to me, "Go and take a look at yourself in the mirror."

Looking at myself in the mirror, I instantly recognized that something had changed. Physically I was exactly the same, but unbeknownst to me, the Lord was changing my heart. I loved how I saw myself and realized then that God was not changing my circumstances.

He was changing me!

I understand now that this was the beginning of my years of going through the valley. I was embarking on more than twenty long years of disciplining, training, and pruning. God was laying down deep, healthy roots to form a strong foundation in Him. God was going to process all of the hurt and pain I had been through to build my character and transform me. It would be a painful journey filled with relapses and self-doubt, but as always, the Lord was patient with me.

As painful as it was, and as much as I complained and argued with the Lord, those years were most crucial in my transformation to the person I am today.

ON THE PATH TO WHOLENESS

In 1986 the Lord led me to attend a Pentecostal church. Every Sunday, as I listened to the word of God being preached, I cried profusely. Unknown to me, it was the Holy Spirit ministering to me. Crying felt like a cleansing feeling. This went on for well over a year. Little did I know the amazing plans the Lord had in store for me.

Being part of that church exposed me to many women's ministries and women's groups. I watched women closely, not knowing that they were mentoring me. They were my role models. The ladies appeared to have everything I desperately wanted—happiness, self-confidence, and the ability to express themselves well. I pretended to talk and act like them, and their opinions soon became my opinions, and I even adopted some of their mannerisms. I had become adept at hiding how terribly wounded I was at every facet of my life.

While some people may have thought that I was normal, I knew differently. I had so many unanswered questions, such as, "What is wrong with me? Why am I so fearful and insecure? Why can't I be like other women? If I'm trying to be like them, then who am I?"

My deepest fear was that I would never change, that I could never change, and would be stuck the way I was—that I would be stuck being me.

I went to church faithfully every Sunday and also to the midweek service. I attended all of the adult Sunday school classes and was exposed to every sermon and every teaching. It was a mystery to me that not one word of God was mentally retained. I became acutely aware of this when, immediately after a sermon was preached, a lady commented on some of the points of the sermon that influenced her. It amazed me that she remembered so much of what was shared just a few minutes ago. My mind was blank. It was frustrating to not recall a single word that was preached. I listened intently to the word of God as it was shared, but as soon as it was over, every word that I heard was gone. Nothing stayed in my memory. I couldn't share with anyone the message of salvation even though it was heard hundreds of times. In fact, it puzzled me when people responded to the call of salvation. I wondered what they were responding to. (It would be more than ten years later when I would finally be able to comprehend the beautiful message of salvation. It happened when the Lord healed me of the trauma of my father's rejection, but that was still a long way away.)

It was a confusing season for me. I felt the strong hand of the Lord guiding and directing me as never before, yet life was still hard. Coping with day-to-day living and my emotional turmoil did not change, but I was growing spiritually. I was learning about God the Father, God the Son, and God the Holy Spirit and developing a deeper, intimate relationship with Him.

The demonic essences intensified in that their condemning voices were louder and more intimidating. I also felt they were trying to pull me down into a dark pit of depression. There were many days when a heavy weight would come upon me, and I would not be able to get out of bed. One evening God sovereignly set me free from the demonic grip on my life. I was walking toward my car in the parking lot of my church after attending a Bible study when I saw, with spiritual eyes, four huge trees that sprung forth from me. I then saw a massive gigantic hand knock down the four trees that were attached to me. It was the hand of the Lord. His hand grabbed a tree, and with one swift pull, the tree and the roots came out of me—from my chest, my heart, and my stomach. I felt as well as saw the long, gnarly, entangled dark roots come out of me. One after another, the Lord, in four easy moves, pulled the trees and all of their roots out. It made a radical difference in my life—the condemning demonic voices were gone and any vestige of depression was forever gone. My insecurities, fears, and other issues were still intact, but it was like being in a wheelchair for decades and now I was able to walk with crutches. For the next ten years I walked in such freedom that I thought I was healed.

But I was wrong. I did not understand the depths of the wounds and scars that had been suppressed since childhood.

There was more to come, so much more. The battle had just begun.

In the fall of 1992, the Lord spoke to me. "I want you to learn about inner healing and deliverance." These terms were unfamiliar to me, so I asked people in the church the meaning of these words. They were not sure either.

Shortly thereafter, the Lord directed me to the Vineyard churches. It was there that I learned about the teachings of John and Paula Sandford, founders of

The Elijah House. Some of their teachings were about dealing with powerful ungodly influences I had not heard of before:

1. Inner vows—promises we make to ourselves as children, such as, "I will never be like my mother."
2. Bitter root judgments—judging others for how they treated us.
3. Bitter root expectancies—expecting the worst, expecting failure or rejection.
4. Generational curses—sins and hurts passed down from one generation to the next.

These teachings were absolutely life changing for me. I learned that inner vows and bitter root judgments are closely linked and how the Bible teaches us that we will be judged as we judge others. Matthew 7:1–2: "Judge not, that you be not judged. For with what judgment you judge, you will be judged; and with the measure you use, it will be measured back to you."

Well, I judged my parents, my siblings, my teachers, and anyone who did not act as I expected them to. I also made inner vows never to be like them, never to be angry, mean, unforgiving, unloving, or bitter, which may sound noble. But it was with a judgmental, critical, angry, and resentful heart. I had to repent of these judgments and vows and to forgive all those who had offended me.

Bitter root expectancies are linked to bitter root judgments and show how our thoughts and words can be powerful. We sometimes expect the worse, or expect to be rejected, or expect failure. Job 3:25: "For the thing I greatly feared has come upon me, And what I dreaded has happened to me."

The Bible teaches that generational curses go down the family line three and four generations. Exodus 34: 6–7: And the Lord passed before him and proclaimed, "The Lord, the Lord God, merciful and gracious, long-suffering, and abounding in goodness and truth, keeping mercy for thousands, forgiving iniquity and transgression and sin, by no means clearing the guilty, visiting the iniquity of the fathers upon the children and the children's children to the third and the fourth generation." Even though I was not involved in it, all the ancestral idol worship that occurred during my growing up years affected me. For instance, I almost drowned twice. I had three accidents that resulted in head injuries. The many car accidents, the unusual family divisions, and the demonic terror that I faced for over sixty years were all the consequences of the ancestral idol worship. It was like opening the door to the demonic realm.

Discovering there was so much more to learn stirred up my hunger for more knowledge about the things of God.

At this point in my life, I was still enjoying the freedom that lasted ten years. The joy of the Lord was as strong as ever and was enabling me to function even with all my issues, like fears, insecurities, nervousness, anxieties, and feelings of worthlessness. I did not know the root cause of my issues yet. I did not know that my life could be any better. I had His joy. I had His presence. What more could there be?

I was so very wrong—there was amazingly more to come.

In 1994 I was privileged to be part of the Toronto Airport Christian Fellowship Church, (TACF). I attended the church prior to and after the Holy Spirit ignited the leadership and congregation. Like many others there in the beginning, I did not understand what was happening. People were falling to the floor after receiving prayer. People were making all sorts of strange sounds. Some had uncontrollable laughter—there was total wreckage all over the place. This was all new to me.

I dismissed it believing that this was not from God. The Lord kept bringing me back to these meetings three to four times a week. I could not stay away. Then people started to give their testimonies of physical healing, emotional healing, healing of relationships, and most of all, spiritual healing. Every week, thousands of people came from all over the world to be touched by God, and many left changed by the power of the Holy Spirit. A true revival was in effect, and thousands of people became witness to God's glory. The evidence of God's transformational power overcame my suspicious nature, and I embraced this spiritual phenomenon.

As I battled to overcome my shyness and insecurity, the Lord moved me to apply to serve as part of the prayer team at TACF. The function of the prayer team was to pray for people who lined up for prayer after the services were over. Although I was nervous, it was comforting to know that we would receive training first and be taught the guidelines of praying for the many visitors who came through the church doors.

One weekend there was a conference underway, and John and Paula Sandford were the keynote speakers. It was held at a hotel because the church was too small to hold the thousands of people who had registered. After the service, hundreds went for prayer, and of course there were not enough people on the prayer team to meet the need, so conference leaders asked me. I was shocked. I wasn't ready yet. I hadn't had any training or even instructions. And now I was being asked to pray for people. Fearful and insecure, I walked to the front of the room. I felt inundated, but somehow my feet got me there.

When the Lord puts you in the water, oftentimes he doesn't put you in the kiddie pool first. He throws you right into the deep end like He did when He asked Moses, who stuttered, to speak to Pharaoh. So I swam in the deep water as I positioned myself to start to pray for the stream of people who were coming to the front of the room. My person catcher was in place in case the person being prayed for happened to fall under the power of the Holy Spirit—or some refer to it as "gets slain in the spirit." There was no backing out.

A man stood in front of me expecting me to pray for him. When I looked at him, I couldn't believe it. It was none other than John Sandford, the keynote speaker—a tall man, well over six feet. I saw him as a giant of a man both physically and spiritually. I, on the other hand, am only four feet ten inches. Even if I wasn't intimidated to pray for him, I didn't know how. My first thought was, No way, I couldn't pray for him. Then I thought to run away or maybe have someone else pray for him. I looked around for a way out and to reposition myself or to pray for someone else instead. But John was squarely in front of me, and there was a pillar behind me, someone to the left of me, and a ledge to my right. I knew then this was God's way of making me jump into the deep end of the pool. Having no alternative, I stretched my hands out, and as I touched his outstretched hands, I began to pray for him. The Holy Spirit touched him, and he fell back onto the catcher. The next person up was John's wife,

Paula. I placed my hands on her hands and began to pray, and she too fell in the power of the Holy Spirit.

The next day, John Sandford shared his testimony of what the Holy Spirit did that affected his life when I prayed for him. This was the launching of my ministry as a prayer minister at the Toronto Blessing church.

The Holy Spirit could and would indeed use a truly broken vessel like me.

As John shared, even though I do not recall his testimony, I knew the Lord wanted to encourage me and let me know that such happenings were not about me, but they were all about Him and what He wanted to accomplish through people who will say yes to Him. I felt a sense of exuberance because I was exactly where God wanted me to be, and I was fulfilling His call.

Over the next few years, I was privileged to pray for numerous people who came internationally to visit the Toronto Blessing church. At the same time, I received some healing also. I was completely healed of chronic fatigue. Some (though not all) of my fears and shame left. I began to feel more confident and secure in the person I was. Most importantly I felt drawn closer to God.

The first time the Holy Spirit touched me power-fully frightened me. I was at TACF praying for a pastor when all of a sudden, I felt the Holy Spirit come upon me with such force and power that I quickly ended my prayer with the pastor. I promptly ran out of the church building and hurried home. Once at home, I knelt on my hands and knees before God for hours. Like the prophet Isaiah, I cried out to God, as in Isaiah 6:5: "Woe is me, for I am undone! Because I am a man of unclean lips; And I dwell in the midst of a people of unclean lips; For my eyes have seen the King, the Lord of hosts." The presence of God was so powerful that I felt like I would explode or burst. It was almost more than I could handle. I am grateful and humbled by the Lord that this was to be the first of many times when I would experience the awe and wonder of His power.

SUPPRESSED EMOTIONS SURFACE

In 1995 I attended a nine-week course on inner healing and deliverance. Here I learned that sometimes, people are in need of deliverance from different strong-holds, like the spirit of rejection, or the spirit of anger, or the spirit of lust. People can be held in bondage to these things, no matter how hard they try to free themselves, until the Lord delivers them from these spirits. Years ago, when the Lord pulled those "trees" from me, I experienced a deliverance from the condemning voices and from the spirit that would pull me into depression.

The location for this course was out in the peaceful countryside, away from city life. It was, and still is, a wonderful retreat center. There were fifty-five students in all, and we stayed in the dormitory during the entire nine weeks. I went there with the intention of learning how to better equip myself to help others, not knowing I was the one who needed help. I believed God had healed me and that I was in a good place and sure, I still had my struggles, but I felt okay.

I did not know that the childhood abuse, neglect, and rejection had piled up layers of pain buried deep inside me. I assumed my fears and insecurities would always be part of my life and that I just needed to learn to live with them. I still struggled with sleepiness. Throughout the course, staying awake during the day took great effort even though I slept well at night. I took naps during lunch breaks, dinner breaks, and even the half-hour breaks in between classes. I paid attention to the speakers like I did the sermons at my church every week, but I could barely capture or remember what I was being taught.

On the first day of the nine-week course, the speaker must have taught about rejection and abandonment. I only recall his invitation to those who had experienced rejection and abandonment to stand; he wanted to pray for us. I stood up, not thinking for a moment that I had any of these issues. But because I paid a lot of money for that course, I had predetermined to respond to every invitation to make sure I got my money's worth. Besides, prayer could never hurt anyone. I remained unaware that the constant rejections of my family were the root of the emotional conflicts in my life. The speaker began to pray for us as a group, and I don't know what happened—I fell on the floor and was wailing and screaming as he prayed over us. Uncontrollable and clueless as to what was happening, because this behavior was out of the ordinary for me, I felt the pain of losing my father's love all over again.

The first big loss had left me bereft when I was six, and the loss continued as I grew up.

But at that moment, it struck me all in one massive impact, and I could not handle it emotionally. I still missed my dad so much, and my heart was full of remorse and sorrow. The essence of the pain was buried deep within me. The Lord opened up the tomb in which all my childhood pain was kept and intense emotions flooded my senses all at once—in a physically painful way. When I was able to control myself, I was fatigued but hopeful that the Lord would heal me.

God heals some people in an instant. Some can be alcoholics or drug addicts, and when they get saved, God takes away their yearnings for their vices. Others have been traumatized, and God heals their inner conflicts in an instant. It was not instantaneous with me. I didn't understand at the time, but this was the start of another leg of my journey, one of true emotional healing and complete wholeness.

My difficulties escalated because every bit of the painful feelings and emotions I had never dealt with now surfaced. I returned home worse off than when I left. It felt like I had an open bullet wound that was bandaged over, and the bandage was ripped off abruptly. My heart hurt, and I often wondered if it was physical. I cried a lot, and my anxieties sky-rocketed. I tried to take control of my life because it felt like I was losing control. God did not seem able or willing to help me.

Once again, my greatest fear was I was forever stuck and there was no way out.

Shortly after, I sought answers to my dilemma and became involved with a Christian counseling center. While there, I attended many seminars and courses and read many books related to emotional healing. I methodically began connecting the dots of who I was and what I had been through.

I learned that God created and designed children to be loved, nurtured, cared and provided for, and made to feel safe and secure in their surroundings. Children learn about communication, relationships, friendships, and the basic tools to live life through parents, teachers, and people they encounter.

The revelation of God's perfect will for children was a pivotal moment for me.

It was an epiphany to know that not receiving from my parents and siblings what God intended caused me to be crippled emotionally.

I learned about childhood traumas, emotional abuse, spiritual abuse, neglect, rejection, abandonment, and also about the potent power and love of God, who wants us to live in wholeness. It was a shock for me to learn how I was shaped and impacted by my childhood experiences.

At last, my questions were answered as to how my identity was developed and formed.

Most importantly, I learned about forgiveness—not the way the world forgives, but the way God forgives. I had to come to grips with the burning anger in my heart toward my mother. I had hated her. I had wished her dead many times after she beat me without provocation, scolded me mercilessly, and took out her anger on me when I was just a little girl. And when I grew up, it was me who had to tend to the needs of a mother I despised.

The founder and director of the counseling center, Art Zeilstra, saw potential in me. I was adamant he was mistaken. The Lord used him to push me and stretch me.

He believed I could speak and teach publicly. This was too far out of my radar range.

I refused and wished he would leave me alone.

"How can I possibly speak before a group of people?"

"I know you can do it, because God will equip you," Art said.

"Why would anyone want to hear me speak?"

His answer was always, "I know you can do it."

"Me, of all people, speaking in public?"

"Yes, you of all people."

"Art, what do you see in me? What makes you think I can do it?"

Art responded that he saw in me a potential to rise up above the limitations that I placed upon myself. I was not convinced. If he knew who I really was, he would know how mistaken he was.

The idea was absurd. I grew up in a house where no one spoke. My upbringing prevented me from developing even basic skills of communication. I was often tongue tied when talking to just one person. Finding the correct words to express myself was challenging. Plus, I was still trying to find a way to get rid of the emotional baggage that was weighing me down.

But eventually under Art's guidance and direction, I stepped out, albeit reluctantly. Initially he provided the opportunity to share a few words. Little by little, I progressed from there. I hated it, but Art persisted, though I made it difficult for him. Like the Israelites, I murmured and complained constantly. Art had such an unshakable faith in me, he was like a Barnabas to me, and that was how I often referred to him.

When I looked at the mirror, I saw an empty person staring at me. I did not see any talents, or even a spark or a hint of potential. In spite of all the miraculous healing I had received from Jesus, in my heart I did not believe that even He could bring me to a place of peace and wholeness. My mountains were too big for God to move.

God would prove otherwise.

GOD MOVES MOUNTAINS

I remember hearing the "Father Loves You" message for the first time in 1995. The essence of God's love captured my attention. I was enthralled by it. I wanted to absorb every word spoken by the speaker, but sadly, as soon as he finished his captivating message, it was totally gone. Not only did I have this issue with words I heard, but also with words I read, such as the Bible, faith-based books, different forms of literature, instructions, and even road signs! It wasn't that I was illiterate. I could read, albeit at the pace of a six-year-old. It was just that words didn't sink in and stay with me. The same problems I had during elementary school.

Comprehending details that should not have been challenging, whether written or verbal instructions, proved nearly impossible. As a result, I ruined a lot of clothes, washing what should be dry cleaned, washing wool clothes in hot water, or mixing different colors with white clothes.

As you can imagine, forgetting instructions and being unable to decipher road signs meant challenges and frustrations when driving anywhere. Seeing road signs—east, west, north, south, exit, and detour—did not register with me. It was as if my eyes were disconnected from my brain. Not understanding the meaning of simple road signs often resulted in driving in the wrong direction.

Driving was like entering into a maze—I would circle the place I wanted to get to before I actually got there.

To make matters worse, my sense of direction was (and is) awful. I got lost easily. For example, after driving into a gas station to fill up on gas, I could never remember which exit I needed to take to continue on my journey. I would randomly take an exit from the gas station, and driving along, I would eventually figure out if I took the right exit. When at a restaurant, if I needed to find the restroom, usually my daughters directed me and then guided me back to my table. One time, I was in a restaurant and the restroom was within sight of my table, but to get to the restroom, I had to maneuver around tables and chairs. It was easy enough, and I should have had no problem finding my way back. Wrong. I could not figure how to get back to my table. I froze. Though embarrassed, I had to ask someone to help me. I still get lost if I walk around an unfamiliar neighborhood.

Also, when driving a car, anxiety often overwhelmed me. I was riddled with fears of getting into an accident or hitting someone and causing someone else serious injury. Thoughts plagued me—like my tires were going to blow up and cause my car to careen out of control. Many times, upon arriving at my destination, my anxiety level would be so high that I would sit in the car in order to compose myself. Overly cautious, I drove slowly and never kept up with the flow of traffic or the speed limit. Changing lanes pushed the panic button and forced me into prayer. "Lord, keep all the cars away from me." He did just that on many occasions.

One day the Lord spoke to me about getting involved with a downtown outreach program that catered to the homeless. I argued with God, not about the work, but about the drive—it meant driving into the heart of the metropolis of Toronto. In order to get there, I would have to drive on a certain highway I had always avoided because of the traffic. God was asking for the impossible this time. I gave Him all my reasons why I couldn't do it, hoping He would change His mind, but He never did change His mind. He still doesn't when He wants me to do something I don't want to do. Finally agreeing, and with fear and trembling, I drove to the outreach center. Needless to say, I was praying intensely the entire way. Reluctantly, I continued to do it again and again and again, navigating my way on the dreaded highway. Sometimes I did it twice a week. On more than one occasion, when the outreach center closed at around eleven at night, I offered to drive some volunteers home rather than see them take the bus late at night. Out of the corner of my eye, I could see the expression of disbelief on the person next to me, who must have been wondering, "What is this crazy woman doing on the road?" My little car, with a stressed-out woman gripping the wheel tightly, crawled along the busy highway while vehicles whizzed by on the left and the right.

Many months later, I noticed a peace and a calmness while driving. It was a new sensation—to drive and not be filled with anxiety and panic. I no longer had to pray profusely for protection. The Lord in His love and mercy did what I never dreamed possible...He removed the anxieties and panic that tormented me while behind the wheel.

All the irrational thoughts disappeared too!

I now zip along highways or freeways and drive the speed limit. At times I even exceed the speed limit! In recent years I have been able to pick up or drop off people at the airport—something I thought I would never do because of the traffic, exits, and confusing signage. The ability to navigate the airport has been another huge mountain the Lord has provided me victory over. It is so exhilarating to drive in this new freedom.

Another area God worked on was my shyness and fear of people. Sometimes at church, God would say, "Go and introduce yourself to that person." As usual, I moaned and groaned when I heard the Lord tell me do something I dreaded. So much easier to do nothing, to just hide. God forced me to battle my tendency to run or shy away. It was time to persevere and push through and pull down another stronghold that had gained a foothold in my life. It was not an easy process and years passed before I conquered this mountain. I had made an inner vow not to be seen, which I had long forgotten. Being invisible meant not interacting with people, and if I didn't interact with people, they couldn't hurt me. This vow protected me. I repented of the inner vow and chose to trust God more. He patiently walked me through the necessary steps to freedom from yet another stronghold.

I have yet to win an argument with God, for which I am grateful. I am thankful that the Lord persisted and that He did not give up on me, because I would have given up on me a long time ago.

BREAKTHROUGH!

One day the Lord led me to an older couple for prayer. I shared my struggles about reading the Bible and retaining and understanding what I read. I wanted to read signs on the road so I would not drive around in circles, and to remember and comprehend the sermons that were preached in church. The couple was so overwhelmed that they thought they could not really help me. They told me that they had taken the Elijah House course from John and Paula Sandford's ministry, and they had attended a nine-week school on healing and deliverance. Yes, that same course I had taken years ago where God uncovered the entire trauma of my childhood—trauma and emotional pain that I was still dealing with. They explained that was the extent of their knowledge in the area of emotional healing. They were still willing to pray for me, but they felt my problems might have been over their heads. Two ladies sat in and interceded while they prayed for me. After about two minutes of prayer, the pain that I had only felt during the nine-week course resurfaced. I screamed and wailed as agony washed over me again like a tidal wave. I was brought back again to the raw emotion of being rejected by my father. I cried like a little girl who just wanted to hug her daddy. My anguish was audible in my cry as I felt my heart break over and over, and as I suffered through years of solitude and loneliness. I cried like I had never cried before for over an hour. This time, God let me get it all out. Layers of my pain, sorrow, guilt, remorse, anger, frustration, and fear were cried out. When I could finally stop crying, I was emotionally, physically, and spiritually exhausted.

Praise God for His goodness and mercy, because that day marked my life. Finally God went to the core of my being and uprooted everything the enemy had installed there to keep me emotionally bound and from truly getting to know God.

The transformation was instant and phenomenal. At long last, I understood and retained information I read. I recalled sermons and comprehended what I had heard.

I knew and understood the Gospel message—the salvation message was now clear to me. It felt as if a huge piece of me had been missing, and God put it back in its original place. As I progressed in my healing journey, I discovered I had to learn the life and social skills I should have learned as a child. Previously unable to read at the pace of an adult, I was now able to progress in stages. I came to understand why children who experience trauma dissociate from the world; at times, it's just too painful. My challenges could not be overcome without the Lord. In certain areas of my life I was like a little girl who only knew how to crawl. Still, I was happy because the lid had been lifted, and eventually I would be able to walk, and then I would be able to run.

CHAPTER EIGHT

WORSHIP

*I*n the year 2000 the Lord instructed me to stop seeking help through counselors. I wondered why but thought He would eventually bring others to help me. He directed me to spend time with Him, to give Him one hour of my time every night. Although still struggling in various areas of my life and facing constant financial worries and challenges, I was led not to ask Him for anything, not for myself and not for my children. I was to totally rely on Him, trusting that He knew my struggles and my needs and would provide the resources if I just focused on worshipping Him. In my wildest imagination, I did not believe the Lord would really bring me to a place of wholeness and stability. But I had no choice but to try to do things His way.

What made this even harder was that the Lord wanted me to spend an hour with Him at three o'clock in the morning. With the sleepiness problems I still had, waking up at three to do anything was physically hard. I'm at my worst at that time of night; all I can think of is sleep. The first year was extremely difficult. As I tried to worship, my heart was exposed for what it was. It seemed like my heart was stone cold. I would have to force myself to enter into a state of worship. Many, many times I gave up, but then I tried again. Usually, my mind wandered off and the hour flew by. Although I loved the Lord and knew His presence since I was a child, I had not been a true worshipper. My time with God would be dominated by requests for my needs and the needs of others. The Lord was teaching me to just minister to Him, to seek first the kingdom of heaven, trusting that everything would fall into place.

Progress was slowly made during the second year. I did ask the Lord for two things. The first was to give me the heart of King David, the psalmist. He loved the Lord with his whole heart, and I wanted to strip away anything in my heart that hindered my worship. The second request I took from Ezekiel 36:26–27: "I will give you a new heart and put a new spirit within you; I will take the heart of stone out of your flesh and give you a heart of flesh. I will put My Spirit within you and cause you to walk in My statutes, and you will keep My judgments and do them."

As I continued to worship the Lord at three in the morning into my third year, I started to feel His presence. I felt Him touching me. It wasn't a dramatic blast— more of a subtle touch. It slowly dawned on me that He was healing me, as I noticed my attitudes were improving and anger and impatience slowly dissipating.

As I worshipped, the Lord was transforming my mind. I saw my mother through His eyes and considered the intensity of pain she had suffered. I had been self-focused on the injustices happening to me and never understood her inability to cope, until the Lord transformed my mind and my heart. One night, the hatred and anger I had toward her disappeared from the recesses of my being. She had died many years prior, and she never knew how sorry I became for never loving her and for my lack of compassion toward her. Still, the Lord healed that deep wound, and He filled the hole that was once a chasm and filled it with His love.

Since then, the hours of worshipping the Lord at three in the morning—feeling His sweet presence, being wrapped in His love—have been the most treasured moments of my life. Over the course of many years, the Lord established a strong foundation and the excess baggage slowly but surely vanished. The Lord even touched areas I did not realize needed healing. Jehovah Rapha (the Lord your healer) healed me of numerous insecurities—self-deprecating thoughts, feelings of worthlessness, self-hatred, fear of the dark, fear of sudden movements or noise—gone. He freed me from debilitating thoughts of hopelessness, self-condemnation, shame, guilt, rejection, abandonment, and so much more. He strengthened my inner being.

He set me free for no other reason but that He loves me.

Ephesians 3:16–21 (NIV):

I pray that out of his glorious riches he may strengthen you with power through his Spirit in your inner being, so that Christ may dwell in your hearts through faith. And I pray that you, being rooted and established in love, may have power, together with all the Lord's holy people, to grasp how wide and long and high and deep is the love of Christ, and to know this love that surpasses knowledge—that you may be filled to the measure of all the fullness of God.

Spending time with the Lord, ministering to Him, loving Him, and thanking Him have changed every aspect of my life. I believe worship has been the most significant key to my healing, to unlimited blessings, and to favor with God and with man. There are testimonies of many people who also have experienced their lives changed and transformed as they pursued the Lord daily in praise and worship.

I must say, it was not an easy journey; the road was long and hard. As God removed each layer of anguish, more emotional pain kept surfacing. My life resembled a tangled web, and I could not see my way out of it. The only thing that worked was waiting on the Lord, persevering in seeking His face, and worshipping Him. Like the potter and the clay, he was shaping me—the Lord knew me better than I knew myself. He knew the potential He had laid within me would have lain dormant had the Lord not directed and guided me. Jeremiah 29:11 (NIV): "'For I know the plans I have for you,' declares the Lord, 'plans to prosper you and not to harm you, plans to give you hope and a future.'"

I am so thankful for my daughters Valerie and Lynn. They have been instrumental in my journey of healing. They pushed me in areas where I needed a push. Many times they would insist that I face my fears rather than run from them. As hard as it was for me to hear, they would speak the truth to me. At times, when I lacked the strength or courage to do something—something that I would not have done on my own—I would do it for them. It was not easy for them being raised by a single mother who did not know where she was going and often didn't know what she was doing. I am so grateful to God that not only them, but all of my children—Victor, Vincent, Vernon, Virginia, and Rosanne—have all been supportive. I treasure them in my heart for not giving up on me and loving me. They have all survived my craziness, my dysfunctions, my fears, and my anxieties. They are the family I never had as a child, and where there was a void, they added the warmth so desperately needed.

My sister, Sucainna, died when she was sixty-three years old. She suffered for many decades with rheumatoid arthritis. Sadly, she never found the peace, happiness, and fulfillment she sought. Billy died at age fifty-nine. He became mentally challenged when he was in his early thirties. He drowned in a river after he had a seizure, which he was prone to having. I had lost contact with him when I left Montreal. My brother Raymond, now in his eighties, still lives with the same unhappiness that we all grew up with. It pains me that my parents, my uncles, Sucainna, and Billy never met Jesus. Raymond is often in my prayers, and I have faith and hope that he too will come to know the peace and joy that can only come through Christ Jesus.

Amazingly, my little brother, Tommy, is doing well in spite of the fact that Billy and Raymond had never accepted him. He was brought up in the same dysfunctional home with irrational jealousies and destructive behaviors. Tommy managed to grow up to be an intelligent and talented man. It has been a joy for me to see him as a devoted husband and father, living a life of contentment and happiness.

My healing journey is ongoing. It will continue until my pilgrimage on earth is over. God continues to stretch me. You may already have figured out that I complained, murmured, and protested a lot with the Lord, yet He never gave up on me. In fact, He is relentless in His desire for us to know Him more and to know His perfect plans for us. The Lord of the universe never ceases to amaze me. I have come to realize that just when we think we have gone as far as we can go, God has much more in store for us. Our potential is limitless.

Today, by the grace of God, I am in a ministry of praying for people. I also teach and speak to small groups. Me, the girl who didn't talk and was never talked to. My life should have ended up different, but God... God showed up. He changed my course. He gave me a new song to sing. He turned my sorrow into joy. He took what the enemy intended for bad and turned it into good. I was not aware of His limitless potential for me.

In writing this book, yet another journey has begun. I am excited because He knows the plans He has for me, and they are good, so very good.

My life journey has been full of surprises. There were a lot of tears, but also a lot of laughter. I passed through some valleys but also had my sunny days on mountain-tops. It certainly has not been boring.

I used to live with many regrets, many "what ifs":

What if that customer never asked me to kiss my dad? How wonderful would it have been to grow up having a great relationship with my dad, enjoying his laughter and love for me. Instead of dwelling on that, I think of the wonderful times I did have with him, however short they were.

What if my sister and older brothers would have understood and accepted me? How great would it have been to work with them in the restaurant? To share life experiences with each other, laugh together, joke together, and to be supportive of each other?

What if my mother was not an alcoholic? We could have had a wonderful mother-daughter relationship.

I am sorry to say that although I loved God, I was also mad at Him for not rescuing me earlier. Why did I have to go through all the pain? I spent so many years just trying to survive, as if I were thrown in the ocean of life without a life jacket and with no one to teach me how to swim.

I thank God for changing me from the inside. He has brought me to a different place, a much better place. My own experiences have allowed me to connect with people who are also wounded and broken. They know I can identify with their suffering. They see what God has done in my life, and maybe it gives them hope that He will do the same for them. When I see the powerful way the Comforter and the mighty Counselor heals people, it erases all my "what ifs." I am eternally grateful that You would use little old me, a vessel that is still broken in some areas. Your mercies certainly endure forever.

If you have read this book, I want you to know that God loves you. There is nothing that you have gone through that He can't make right. There is no devil, no society, and no carnal desire that is stronger than the

Lord of Hosts. Let Him in. He loves you. He loves you
so much.

II Samuel 7:18–22:

> Then King David went in and sat before the
> Lord; and he said: "Who am I, O Lord God? And
> what is my house, that You have brought me this far?
> And yet this was a small thing in Your sight, O Lord
> God; and You have also spoken of Your servant's
> house for a great while to come. Is this the manner of
> man, O Lord God?" Now what more can David say
> to You? For You, Lord God, know Your servant. For
> Your word's sake, and according to Your own heart,
> You have done all these great things, to make Your
> servant know them. Therefore You are great, O Lord
> God. For there is none like You, nor is there any God
> besides You, according to all that we have heard with
> our ears.

Psalm 52:8–9 (NIV):

> But I am like an olive tree flourishing in the house
> of God;
> I trust in God's unfailing love forever and ever.

For what You have done I will always praise You in
the presence of Your faithful people.

And I will hope in Your name, for Your name is good.

QUESTIONS
TO REFLECT UPON

1. What are some of your dreams? What are some of your goals?

2. Do you feel God is not hearing your prayers? Has this book helped you to know that God does hear your prayers?

3. Do you have difficulty knowing He has never left you nor forsaken you?

4. What fears and anxieties are you dealing with right now in your life?

5. Which sections in this book, *But God...* can you use to help you deal with your fears and anxieties?

6. Do you struggle with self-worth?

7. Is it difficult sometimes to believe that you are worthy of Jesus' love and healing?

   Has this book encouraged you to believe that you are worthy of Jesus' love and Jesus pursues you and wants to heal you?

8. What do you think about Mimi allowing the Lord to use her for His purposes in spite of her brokenness? Did that surprise you about her? Did that surprise you about the Lord? Can you allow the Lord to use you right now where you are at?

9. Which chapter or section of the book struck the deepest chord in your heart, and why? Has this book led you to make a decision for Christ? Has this book led you to seek the Lord for healing?

10. Has this book helped you to know that God has placed within each one of us gifts and talents, and that it is His desire to help us uncover these hidden treasures?

    May you dare to dream again.

CPSIA information can be obtained at www.ICGtesting.com
Printed in the USA
LVOW09s0350200215

427576LV00001B/1/P